Italian Ars Nova Music

Johannes de Florentia, *from the Squarcialupi Codex, fol. 195v*

Viola L. Hagopian

Italian Ars Nova Music

A BIBLIOGRAPHIC GUIDE TO MODERN EDITIONS AND RELATED LITERATURE

Second Edition, Revised and Expanded

University of California Press
Berkeley, Los Angeles, London

University of California Press
Berkeley and Los Angeles, California
University of California Press, Ltd.
London, England

To John and Caryl

Contents

Foreword

to the First Edition

x

ıoi1
)rlw
ɳɘɈ
:oꓷ
I
rɓw
lo'ɪ
{ɕɈI
Ɉɳɘ
ɳiɾ1
Ɉiꓷ
lɘw
'ɪɘꓷ

The music of fourteenth century Italy has attracted so many scholars both here and abroad, especially during the past three decades, that the enthusiasm they have generated perhaps matches the ardor and zeal of the early trecentists themselves when they first began to set their *madrigali amorosi* to *soave et dolci melodie*. A fascinating period was the Trecento, and, moreover, equally fascinating to the cultured fourteenth and fifteenth century gentleman collector, for many of the compositions were copied and preserved in libraries beyond the Italian border.

Thanks to the ever-growing number of philologists, musicologists, and musicologically trained performers, who have dedicated themselves to the Italian Ars Nova, we have been provided with excellent critical editions and fine recordings. But musicological research continues. Much has happened since the pioneering works of Johannes Wolf and Friedrich Ludwig first appeared at the beginning of the twentieth century and opened the vault to the fourteenth-century treasures of Italian music. Since then many papers have been read before national and international musicological congresses; articles have been published on specific practices; translations of fourteenth-century treatises are now available as are studies on Italian notation, composers, and their music; manuscript inventories have appeared in our musicological journals and simplified their identification; and recently, complete collections have been begun by Nino Pirrotta for the American Institute of Musicology and by Leo Schrade and this writer for Editions de l'Oiseau Lyre.

To these various facets such writers as Heinrich Besseler, Leonard Ellinwood, Kurt von Fischer, Federico Ghisi, Annamarie von Königslow, Susan Le Clercx, Ettore LiGotti, Nino Pirrotta, Gilbert Reaney, Claudio Sartori, Leo Schrade, and myself (to mention but a few) have contributed to the expanding Trecento edifice. In the face of this wealth of informa-

tion concerning the music and literature of this period, we are over-
whelmed yet delighted when still another publication comes to our attention. How to keep the facts straight and in their proper niches has no
doubt been asked by many a student and teacher.

Fortunately, this situation was foreseen by Viola Hagopian in 1961
when she embarked on the tortuous path and undertook the laborious
role by examining the contents of these publications dealing with the
Italian Trecento. Each item was duly noted, briefly described, and
entered under its proper classification. Once the reader has familiarized
himself with the method of classification, he will certainly find this
bibliography a trustworthy and useful guide, a time-saving tool, and a
welcome addition to Trecento studies. Mrs. Hagopian has indeed ren-
dered a much-needed service to the cause of musicology.

W. Thomas Marrocco
1964

Foreword
to the Second Edition

❧

In eight years, Viola Hagopian's study on Italian Trecento music has reached the coveted status, "out of print." Certainly for the author and the publisher, the publication proved to be a necessary and useful tool; and the University of California Press is to be commended in sensing the need for a second edition. The original purpose of this book remains the same: a bibliography of Italian Ars Nova music.

Since 1964, new sources have come to light, new studies have been published, and new editions of music have appeared. Through the inspired and indefatigable leadership of Professor Kurt von Fischer, the Centro di Studi sull' Ars Nova Italiana del Trecento, in Certaldo, Italy, continues to flourish, thanks to a subvention from the Italian government. That it has become an international center is attested to by the fact that at its last meeting in 1969, scholars from eight countries (including Japan and Poland) presented papers on various aspects of Italian Trecento music. Some refuted or questioned previously accepted notions; others added new data and strength in support of ideas once thought untenable; fresh and often differing interpretations of the entire subject have been expressed; and a more accurate chronology has been determined. The papers have thus filled three volumes—a far cry indeed from the few paragraphs allotted to the Italian Trecento by the Finneys and the Fergusons of the early 1940s.

It must appear to the interested student that an exhaustive inquiry of this magnitude would have penetrated every nook and cranny in the intricate web of Trecento musical practice. Yet, despite the heavy concentration of scholarly activity, there still remain a few crevices that refuse to admit a shaft of light. I am thinking of that bête noire, *musica ficta*, the role of instruments in the performance of the music, the manner of singing with or without embellishments, the meaning of ligatures in a textless tenor part, the large number of compositions still classified as anonymous, and finally, biographical data of many composers whose activities beyond those of their métier are completely unknown to us. Although the last chapter has yet to be written, the chase after these elusive problems continues.

W. Thomas Marrocco
1972

Preface
to the Second Edition

To those familiar with research techniques it is a well-known fact that bibliographies by their very nature are subject to obsolescence, or at best to near obsolescence. This is particularly applicable to the bibliography of the Italian Ars Nova, since this field of music has been the beneficiary of some seventy years of scholarly activity, an activity that continues to gather momentum.

The most important single factor contributing to this accelerated momentum has been the establishment in 1959 of the Centro di Studi sull'Ars Nova Italiana del Trecento, located at Certaldo. In the auspicious first ten years of its life the center has yielded a bonanza of information, yet this is not to say that scholars have not continued to work independently as well. The results of these combined efforts have prompted an updating of this bibliography.

In order to enhance the usefulness of this second edition, the majority of entries have been given a capsule description.

V. L. H.
Spring 1972

Acknowledgments

I recall with gratitude the first of a number of visits to Professor Federico Ghisi in Florence when, in 1962, he kindly read the manuscript of the first edition of this guide and shared generously with me his vast fund of knowledge. It was he who made me acquainted with Certaldo, at the same time recommending that I substitute "Ars Nova" for "Trecento" in the title.

When early in 1967 I began to think seriously of a revised and enlarged second edition of this work, my proposal met with the wholehearted enthusiasm of Dr. W. Thomas Marrocco of the University of California at Los Angeles and of Dr. Vincent H. Duckles, music librarian at the University of California at Berkeley. During the intervening years I incurred a debt to them both, for the latter was always ready with advice concerning the organization of the bibliography, and Professor Marrocco made numerous helpful and generous contributions to my own efforts. He also read the final manuscript in detail with me.

In addition, I am grateful to Mrs. Grete Frugé of the School of Librarianship of the University of California, who made several useful editorial suggestions regarding certain portions of the text.

In the summer of 1971 it was my good fortune to have a meeting with the indefatigable Kurt von Fischer, and in the months that followed I was the fortunate beneficiary of his profound scholarship.

Shortly before this manuscript was delivered to the press, a chance correspondence with F. Alberto Gallo proved fortuitous, for he too made a number of voluntary contributions. These, together with several others, for the most part forthcoming publications, will be found in the Postscript.

Finally, I wish to thank all of the librarians of the great Music Library of the University of California at Berkeley for their sustained help and cooperation.

V. L. H.
Spring 1972

Introduction

SCOPE

The Trecento of Dante, Giotto, Petrarch, and Boccaccio is also distinguished for its musical contribution, namely the awakening and unparalleled flowering of secular vocal music. It was during this period that the love affair between poetry and music, which had its inception with the trovatori and laudesi, came to full fruition. No one has put it more aptly than Nino Pirrotta in referring to "The spring flowers of the Ars Nova." [1] Indeed, these "flowers" represent a yield of some six hundred compositions on popular (*volgare*) texts.

It is the purpose of this bibliographic guide to bring to light, as nearly as possible, the entire output of this musical activity that has become available in modern editions and, in addition, to provide a guide to the literature pertaining to these works, to the manuscripts, and to the composers. Transcribed fragments and fragments of sources in facsimile are excluded. Also excluded are dance forms (istampite, saltarelli, trotti).

It is obvious that a thorough study of Italian Ars Nova music cannot be undertaken without a consideration of both the rich literary background and the theoretical treatises. But because this guide purports to be an in-depth study neither of poetry nor of theory, only major works pertaining to these two areas are cited.

Italian music for our purposes will mean works in the Italian style; this must of necessity include a number of contributions by composers who, like Ciconia and Dufay, though not Italian by birth or heritage, spent a great part of their lives in Italy, thus coming under the Italian influence. It will also apply to works by composers of doubtful origin, such as Egidio, when the style is Italian. On the other hand, works that do not fit this description are excluded, even when composed by Italians, as in the cases of Bartolomeo Brollo, Antonello and Filippo da Caserta, and

---

1. Pirrotta 25, 57.

Matteo da Perugia. Over half a century of papal residence at Avignon (1309–1376) had brought about a close political relationship between France and Italy, with a resultant infiltration of the French style and language into Italy. This is nowhere better exemplified that in the works of Matteo da Perugia and of the two Casertas, which display the characteristics of the French mannerists found at Avignon. Yet the notation is typically fourteenth-century Italian, that is, individual signs are employed for special note values. In some instances, pieces in the Italian style were composed on French texts,[2] while chansons in the French style made use of Italian words.[3] In still other cases, we find a mixture of Italian and Latin, or of Italian and French texts, as in some of the works of Hugo de Lantins and Zachara da Teramo.

It will be observed throughout the following pages that the terms "Trecento" and "Italian Ars Nova" occur interchangeably. Although the shades of difference between these expressions must be left to the text, it must here be pointed out that there is some disagreement among scholars in this area. Kurt von Fischer scrupulously avoids the use of the more recent connotation "Italian Ars Nova," yet Federico Ghisi prefers it. Professor Fano (Fano *4*) defends its application to an entire century of polyphonic activity, which does not coincide literally with the span of the fourteenth century, or Trecento, but extends rather from about 1325 to 1425. We know that the French and Italian Ars Nova shared in common a fresh polyphony, together with a heretofore unknown rapport with the poetry that inspired it. The Italian, while lacking the Gothic style of the French, displayed a far greater capacity for lyricism, and this lyricism was to remain one of its distinguishing characteristics.

On the basis of stylistic analysis, the period under consideration may be divided into three generations. The first consists chiefly of Piero, Giovanni da Cascia (also known as Johannes de Florentia), Jacopo da Bologna, and Vincenzo da Rimini. More difficult to define is the second generation, for many composers in this period are borderline cases. Most certainly to this group belong Gherardello, Donato and Lorenzo da Firenze, and Nicolò da Perugia. On the border of this generation and the third one we find Andrea dei Servi, Bartolino da Padova, Paolo Tenorista, and that most prolific of all Ars Nova composers, Francesco Landini (also known as "Il Cieco"). These composers, particularly Paolo, tend to lean toward the last group. To this third generation, often referred to as the "late Ars Nova" group, belong unequivocally Antonello da Caserta, Bartolomeo Brollo, Bartolomeo da Bononia, Johannes Ciconia, Guil-

---

2. Landini's "Adiu . . ." (Fischer *32, 38*); the anonymous "Quant je voy" (Fischer *32, 38*).
3. Dufay's "Quel fronte . . ."; "Dona i ardenti rari."

laume Dufay, Matteo da Perugia, Zachara da Teramo and Zacherias, CDNP.

Before 1900 this vast treasure mine had remained virtually undiscovered,[4] but at the turn of the century the pioneer studies of Friedrich Ludwig and Johannes Wolf paved the way for the extensive researches that were to follow. It was Wolf's study of mensural notation in 1904 (*Geschichte der Mensuralnotation . . .*) that provided the key to the great body of Trecento music. In 1905 Riemann, too, made his contribution, and Heinrich Besseler commenced his studies in the 1920s. Conspicuous among later scholars are the names of Ellinwood, Fischer, Ghisi, Marrocco, Pirrotta, Reaney, and Schrade, who have brought to light a wealth of new material, and who have not been content with merely transcribing the contents of the manuscripts into modern notation. They have also written extensively on every aspect of this music, and there is little indication of waning interest. Indeed, to the roster of distinguished names may now be added those of Frank D'Accone, F. Alberto Gallo, Ursula Günther, Marie Martinez-Göllner, Nigel Wilkins, and others.

In 1958 Kurt von Fischer (Fischer *33*) surveyed the achievements of over half a century of research, commenting on the momentum this scholarly activity had gathered. The brief interval between his survey and the appearance of the first edition of the present bibliography saw the publication of the Ars Nova papers at the Colloques de Wégimont, the establishment of the Centro di Studi sull'Ars Nova Italiana del Trecento at Certaldo, a continuation of the manuscript studies in *Musica Disciplina,* a second edition of W. Thomas Marrocco's *Fourteenth-Century Italian Cacce,* Leo Schrade's edition of the works of Francesco Landini, and three additional volumes of Nino Pirrotta's distinguished collections, *The Music of Fourteenth-Century Italy.* Between the years 1963 and 1971 there has appeared a fifth volume to the Pirrotta set, while Dr. Marrocco, in undertaking the completion of the l'Oiseau-Lyre *Polyphonic Music of the Fourteenth Century (Italian Secular Music),* has already published volume 6 of the set, with volume 7 and 8 due in 1972. In informing me that the preparation of the remaining three volumes has beeen completed, Professor Marrocco very kindly made available to me the tables of contents of these three volumes, thus enabling me to account for numerous additional transcriptions.

In preparing this bibliographic guide the writings of the above-named

4. Although as early as 1776 Charles Burney (*General History of Music,* 1 [2nd ed. 1935], 625–646) had displayed a keen awareness of it, and Fétis made more than passing comments in 1835 (Fét *1*) and again in 1876 (Fét *3*, 305–315). Somewhat later there followed brief articles: Gandolfi, in *Rassegna nazionale,* 1888; Gandolfi and Wolf in *Nuova musica* between the years 1896–1899. Nor to be overlooked are Gandolfi's comments accompanying his facsimile edition of Florentine music in 1892 (Gandolfi *2*).

scholars have been consulted extensively; and Gustave Reese's *Music in the Middle Ages,* together with Fischer's *Studien zur italienischen Musik . . .* have served as principal starting points for the study. The latter provided a bibliographical guide, and those familiar with the work will now recognize the need for amplification.

The present undertaking provides a composer approach, whereas Fischer's approach, though including a composer index and tabulation by composer, is essentially an approach through text incipit—not without logic, since the composer enjoyed little importance during the Ars Nova period. But in the following centuries, the role of the composer assumed a new importance, and his ever-increasing importance has been accompanied by an increased need for composer guides.

In view of the abundance of literature pertaining to the musical activity of this period, an extensive bibliography is also pertinent. It is hoped that this guide will prove useful to performing musicians and to musicologists alike, by providing ready information on what is available in terms of music and related literature.

It can now be said that within a very short time the transcriptions of this vast body of Trecento music will have been virtually completed, with the possible exception of a handful of illegible fragments.[5] In addition, many problems relating to identity and attribution have now been solved. Yet it is quite possible that scholars will uncover still more of these fourteenth-century treasures, hidden away in some obscure, out-of-the-way manuscripts; for Sacchetti lists other works by composers whose names are already familiar, as well as a number by Jacopo and Giovanni de Gherardello, Ottolino da Brescia, and even one by himself.[6] And LiGotti makes mention of an Albertuccio della Vinota and of one Scochetto.[7]

ARRANGEMENT AND METHOD

The History and Criticism section (pp. 13–74) is divided into ten classified parts. All areas are so closely linked that they often overlap. This is particularly applicable to stylistic analysis, which, because it is diffused throughout the numerous entries, has not been assigned a specific section heading.

A very small number of works cited have not been examined, and these

5. Although this bibliographic guide does not cover sacred works of the period, it is nevertheless fitting to call attention to the announcement of yet another volume in the l'Oiseau-Lyre series *(PMF)*. This consists of transcriptions of Italian sacred music, edited by Kurt von Fischer and F. Alberto Gallo.

6. Fischer *32,* 77–78.

7. LiGotti *5,* 14. See also Pirrotta *14,* 653–654; Burney (op. cit.), 627.

are so indicated with a symbol (#). In such cases, however, they have been included on the strength of their repeated appearance as references and also on the strength of the reputation of their authors. At the same time, in the interests of selectivity and conciseness, some of the material that was examined has been rejected.

All material used is listed alphabetically in Appendix I (page 111). Complete entries are given for each item the first time it is used in the body of the work. Thereafter, it will be referred to by the number assigned to it in Appendix I. For example, Fischer 6 will always denote his "Les compositions à trois voix. . . ." Similarly, Pirrotta 26:I will denote his *The Music of Fourteenth Century Italy*, Vol. I. Symbols have been devised for periodicals, series, and for reference works most frequently used, such as *MGG*. Whenever possible, use has been made of the symbols employed by Reese in the bibliography of *Music in the Renaissance*.

Where no biographical information is indicated, it is to be assumed that the following standard reference works were consulted: Baker, Eitner, Fétis, Grove, *MGG*, Riemann, and Schmidl. The reader is advised to consult bibliographies of all *MGG* articles cited.

The variant forms of composers' names can often prove troublesome. I have preferred the Italian form whenever possible, excepting in the case of those theorists who are generally known by the Latinized form of their names. Provision has been made for the variants in both the composer listings and in the index.

In cases where there is a complete edition of a composer's works or where a substantial number of compositions is found in a single collection, it is listed first. Sources containing other works or other versions follow in alphabetical order.

General Symbols

SYMBOL	MEANING
#	Was not examined.
[Number following work symbol]	Page number, e.g., Wolf *4,* 636. In case of *MGG,* column number.
[Roman numeral (sometimes followed by lower case letter) following an entry]	The section where the entry is abstracted, e.g., "(II)" indicates section on Forms; "(V b)" indicates the section on Manuscript Sources: Major.
no. [followed by a number]	Composition number, e.g., Marrocco *3;* no. 2.
[Roman numeral following composer's dates or name]	The generation of Trecento composers to which he most nearly belongs.
*	In the case of literature: important. In the case of transcriptions: complete edition.

Manuscripts and Their Sigla
(with page numbers indicating where each is cited)

∽∾∿

Ber	Berlin, Deutsche Staatsbibl. der Stiftung Preussischer Kulturbesitz, cod. lat. 4°523. Fragment 58, 85, 92
BL Q15	Bologna, Civico museo bibliografico musicale, Q15 (olim Liceo musicale 37) (BL) 59–60, 99 n. 92
BL Q16	Bologna, Civico museo bibliografico musicale, Codex Q16 (olim Liceo musicale) 54, 103, *103*
BU	Bologna, Bibl. universitaria 2216 50, 53 n. 42, 60, 83, *130*
Cas	Rome, Bibl. Casatenense, c II, 3 59, 65, 99
Dom	Domodossola, Convento di Monte Calvario, ms. 14, now at Stresa, Collegio Rosmini 44, 60, 80, 102, *103*
Esc	Escorial IV. α. 24 (EscB) 61, *103*
Faenza	Faenza, Bibl. comunale 117 (Fa) (Bonadies) 42, 49–50, 67, 68, *103*, 103
FP	Florence, Bibl. nazionale centrale, Panciatichi 26 (Panc. 26) 5, 13, 38, 51, 52–53, 82, 83, 86, 88, 90, 93, 98
Grot	Grottaferrata, Bibl. della Badia greca E. β. XVI. Fragment 61, 61 n. 50, 86, 88

9

Iv	Ivrea, Bibl. capitolare, cod. 104
	61, 92
Lo	London, British Museum, Additional 29987 (L)
	53, 75, 78, 81, 85, 86, 87, 88, 89, 90, 93, 95, 99, *104*, 104
Luc	Lucca, Archivio di Stato, ms. 184 (Mancini) (Man) (Mn)
	15, 45, 53–55, 65, 76, 77, 78, 80, 81, 90, 95, 100, 101, *104*,
	104, *106*, 106
Man	see Luc
Mod	Modena, Bibl. Estense, α.M. 5,24 (olim. lat. 568) (Est)
	20, 28, 45, 47, 61–62, 78, 94, 101, *104*
NYL	New York, Private Library of Professor Edward E. Lowinsky, now at Chicago. Fragment
	62, 96, *105*
Ostiglia	see RsO
O	Oxford, Bodleian Library Canonici Misc. 213 (O 213)
	43, 62–63, 63 n. 51, 77, 79, 80, 82, 83, 93, 94, 99 n. 92, 101
Oxford, Can. Pat. lat. 229	see PadA
PadA	Padua, Bibl. universitaria, mss. 684 and 1475; also Oxford, Bodleian Library, Can. Pat. lat. 229. Fragments
	35, 63–64
PadB	Padua, Bibl. universitaria, ms. 1115. Fragment
	35, 64, 77, 80, 105
PadC	Padua, Bibl. universitaria, ms. 658. Fragment
	35, 63 n. 52, 64, 80
PadD	Padua, Bibl. universitaria, ms. 1106. Fragment
	44
Parma	Parma, Archivio di Stato. Fragment
	77, 80
PC	Paris, Bibl. nationale, nouv. acq. franç 4379
	80
PerBC	Perugia, Bibl. comunale, ms. 3065 (olim G20). Fragment of Luc
	53–54, 53 n. 41, *106*, 106
Pist	Pistoia, Archivio capitolare del Duomo. Fragment of Luc
	53–54, 53 nn. 41 and 42, *106*, 106
Pit	Paris, Bibl. nationale, fonds italien 568 (P)
	55–56, 56 n. 44, 69, 75, 78, 80, 82, 84, 85, 87, 90, 93, 95, 96,
	96 n. 87, 97, 100, *105*, 105

PR   Paris, Bibl. nationale, nouv. acq. fanç. 6771 (Reina) (R)
                                  42, 56–57, 56 n. 45, 69, 78, 79, 86, 88, 90, *105*, 105

Pz   Paris, Bibl. nationale, nouv. acq. franç. 4917 (P 49)
                                  50, 64, 80, 100, *106*

Rs   Rome, Bibl. Vaticana, Rossi 215 (Rossi)
                     26, 27, 28, 36, 39, 43, 44, 47, 57–59, 69, 86, 93, 98, *107*, 107

RsO   Rome, Bibl. Vaticana, Rossi 215. Ostiglia fragment: "Raccolta Greggiati"
                                  57–58, 107

RU$_1$ Rome, Bibl. Vaticana Urb. lat. 1419
                                  65, *106*

RU$_2$ Rome, Bibl. Vaticana Urb. lat. 1411
                                  65, 80, 83

Sev   Sevilla, Bibl. Colombina, 5 2 25
                                  65, 90, 92

SieA,   Siena, Archivio di Stato. 2 fragments
SieB
                                  65–66, *107*, 107

Sq   Florence, Bibl. Medicea Laurenziana, Palatino 87 (Squarcialupi) (Pal. 87) (FL)
                     13, 21, 25, 28, 35, 35 n. 24, 39, 47, 50–52, 52 n. 38, 75, 79, 82, 84, 85, 87, 88, 90, 93, 95, 96, 100, 101

Str   Strasbourg, ms. 222 C. 22
                                66, 77, 80, 89, 90, 96, 96 n. 86

Tr   Trent, Castello del buon consiglio, 87 (Tr. 87)
                                107, *108*, 108

History and Criticism

⚜

ARS NOVA PERIOD IN GENERAL (I)

Apel, Willi, ed. *French Secular Music of the Late Fourteenth Century.* Cambridge, Mass., Mediaeval Academy of America, 1950. Introduction and Commentary.

An analysis of this period reveals three leading styles: that of Machaut; the "mannerist" style (1370–90); and the "modern," which bridges the gap between mannerism and Dufay's fifteenth-century style. Traits suggesting Italian influences are considered.

Becherini, Bianca. "L'Ars Nova italiana del Trecento: strumenti ed espressione musicale." *Cert* I (1962), 40–56.

A further pursuance of the observations of Riemann, Wolf, Ludwig, and Schering regarding the use of instruments. Particular reference to the *Decamerone*, to the *Paradiso degli Alberti,* to Landini, and to the codices Sq and FP.

————. "Le insegne viscontee e i testi poetici dell'Ars Nova." In *Liber Amicorum Charles Van den Borren,* ed. by Albert Van der Linden. Anvers, Imprimerie Anversois, 1964, 17–25. (IV)

————. "Poesia e musica in Italia ai primi del XV secolo." *Wég* (1959), 239–259.

* Besseler, Heinrich. "Ars Nova." *MGG* I (1949), 702–729.

This study scarcely represents a departure from the author's earlier view (Besseler *11, 13*), and the Trecento is included almost reluctantly under the heading *Ars Nova.* The *Tonwortkunst* is held as the essence of Trecento music, while conceding that often poet and singer were not the same. There was no representative large form resembling the isorhythmic motet; in fact, Italian composers resisted this form. Yet an acquaintance with French works of this period is revealed in their use of the hocket, particularly in accompanying instrumental parts. The caccia and canonic madrigal are derived from the French chace, while the ballata, reaching its highest point of development with Landini, had its roots in the thirteenth-century lauda.

13

The madrigal was to remain a soloistic *Gesangmusik*. In principle it resembles Provençal organum, but now with a free melismatic upper voice
over a quiet tenor. Italian coloratura virtuosity is evident in the works of
Giovanni and Jacopo, and this *Singfreudigkeit* reaches a high point in the
works of the Florentines Gherardello and Lorenzo.

*————. *Die Musik des Mittelalters und der Renaissance*. Potsdam, Aka-
demische Verlagsgesellschaft Athenaion, 1931.

Although the following critical annotations cover only pp. 151–166, "Italien
und der Mittelkreis im Gotischen Zeitalter," it is strongly recommended
that the student begin reading from p. 112 in order to have the background
essential to an understanding of what follows.

In spite of the thesis advanced by some scholars, Italy's surrender and
almost total renunciation of the achitectural grandeur of the northern motet
makes it impossible to consider the Trecento as the herald of a new epoch
in music history. Activity in Italy is no more than a tributary and does not
alter the course of the Gothic mainstream. Nor is the precedence of the
ephemeral madrigal over the French ballade in the least demonstrable. Italy
became active relatively late in music history, and therefore there is little to
assess of its role until the thirteenth century, when the lauda assumed importance. This lauda, particularly that of Francesco d'Assisi and his followers, became the most potent factor leading to the *Trecentokunst*. This is
not to say that there were not other contributing factors, such as the
Provençal troubadour art of the north Italian courts and the *dolce stil
nuovo*. The oldest form of Italian secular polyphony, the two-voiced
madrigal, is derived from Provençal organum and is comparable to the
French ballade. Here is a new base for polyphonic music. In contrast to the
Gothic effort to maintain individuality of voices, the *Trecentokunst* reveals
a "oneness of polyphonic tonal capacity," as demonstrated in the coloratura
upper voice; and the tenor is a true bass in the harmonic sense. The addition of thirds and sixths to this two-part madrigal leads in time to the three-
part madrigal. In contrast to the pathos of the troubadours and the chivalric ideals of the preceding period, here the social milieu is one of courtly
elegance, as exemplified in Boccaccio's *Decamerone*. Perhaps this *Luxuskunst,*
or "jeunesse dorée," explains the inner weakness of the Italian *Trecentokunst*. Even Landini's leadership was marked by a stylistic weakness,
being no more than a luxury product of the nobility, and as a result it
could not maintain itself against the stronger north.

————. "Studien zur Musik des Mittelalters: Neue Quellen des 14. und be-
ginnenden 15. Jahrhunderts." *AfMW* VII (1925), 167–252.

Again the importance of French influence is stressed, and contributing factors are enumerated: French epics, which were known and had been translated (two Tuscan translations of the *Roman de la rose*); art of the Provençal troubadours; influence of French language and literature, as well as
of architecture and sculpture; motet of Notre Dame not unknown in Italy.

————. "Studien. . . ." *AfMW* VIII (1926), 137–258.

This discredits Riemann's hypothesis regarding the date of the *Pomerium,*

for it is felt that it must be later. It is also felt that the madrigal emerges
from the conductus as a pure Italian form and not from accompanied
monody, as Riemann would have it.

Bonaccorsi, Alfredo. "Un nuovo codice dell'Ars Nova: Il Codice Lucchese."
Atti della accademia nazionale dei Lincei, Ser. 8, Vol. I:12 (1948), 539–615.
Distinguishing characteristics of the Italian Ars Nova, with particular reference to the melodic line and to the forms. Problems and theories of performance practice.

Bonaventura, Arnaldo. "Il Boccaccio e la musica." *RMI* XXI (1914), 405–442.
An examination of the *Decamerone* from the musical point of view and a
discussion of the use of instruments.

* ———. *Dante e la musica*. Livorno, R. Giusti, 1904.

———. "Musica e poesia del Trecento italiano." *Musica d'oggi* XVIII (1936),
3–7.
Though, generally speaking, the development of music was not parallel
with but later than that of poetry, yet the alliance and accord between the
two, which reached its peak in the Florentine Ars Nova, coinciding with
the *dolce stil nuovo*, had earlier beginnings with the popularized lauda.

Borren, Charles Van den. "L'Ars Nova." *Wég* (1959), 17–26.
In the abstract, "Ars Nova" could be applied to any manifestation of the
new, from the organum of Notre Dame to twentieth-century *musique
concrète*. The new is always linked to a certain decadence, which sets in
when the old reaches an impasse. As related to the subject in question, the
term "Ars Nova" can be used to convey the idea of fourteenth-century polyphony in a broad sense. How can its sudden appearance in Italy be ex-
plained in the absence of a previous background? Avignon, the perfect
meeting ground between French and Italian, seems the obvious answer,
though there still remain some unresolved questions.

———. "Considérations générales sur la conjonction de la polyphonie italienne
et de la polyphonie du nord pendant la première moitié du XVe siècle."
Institut historique belge de Rome, Bull. XIX (1938), 157–187.

———. *Etudes sur le quinzième siècle musical*. Anvers, De Nederlandsche
Boekhandel, 1941, 120–123.
Brief observations on the late Ars Nova, or "transition" period. Remarks on
some composers must be modified, since their works have now been transcribed.

Bridgman, Nanie. "Les illustrations musicales des oeuvres de Boccaccio dans les
collections de la Bibliothèque nationale de Paris." *Cert* III (1970), 105–130.
Eight plates, together with remarks on musical activity, demonstrate the
high popularity of secular music, and also the use of instruments in performance.

Carapetyan, Armen, ed. Anonimi. *Notitia del valore delle note del canto
misurato*. Rome, American Institute of Musicology, 1957 (*CSM*, 5).

The Florentine "school" of the pre-Medicean period has now gained wide recognition, though its origins and early development have yet to be traced. Its composers have carried polyphonic art to one of its summits, and Landini is likened to Machaut.

Carducci, Giosuè. "Musica e poesia nel mondo elegante italiano del secolo XIV," in his *Studi letterari*. Bologna, Zanichelli, 1929, 301–397.

Cimbro, Attilio. "La musica e la parola dal trecento al cinquecento." *RaM* II (1929), 293–301.
In the fourteenth century, the relationship of words to music differed in France and Italy. In the former, this was sober and calculated, while in the latter, music prevailed over words. Indeed, in Italy there was a musical exuberance. The melismas of the Florentine madrigal infiltrated ecclesiastical music, and the Florentine style exerted considerable influence over the future.

Clercx, Suzanne. "Introduction" [Allocation prononcée au cours de la séance académique d'ouverture des Colloques de Wégimont II, 1955, l'Ars Nova]. *Wég* (1959), 10–13.
By way of an introduction to the Wégimont conference, the chairman recognizes the phenomenon of the Ars Nova as one of those moments in the history of art and human thought when the new appears suddenly, as a sort of mutation. This eloquent spokesman and champion of the French Ars Nova concedes that Italy too played a role; for in the melting pot of Avignon, Italy had been exposed to French influence, yet it remained true to its own tradition, a tradition marked by roots deep in classical antiquity and in the old Mediterranean world.

*————. *Johannes Ciconia*. Bruxelles, Palais des académies, 1960. Vol. I, 16–27, 41–50, 65–79, 82–92, 95–117.
Pages cited apply specifically to Italy, to Ciconia in Italy, and to Ciconia's Italian works (pp. 65–79, manuscripts; pp. 95–117, notation, including Italian notation). Regarding the aspect of chromaticism, reference is made to Marchettus' *Lucidarium* and to Ciconia's *Nova musica*, then to the latter's treatment of *musica ficta*. But for our purposes the unique value of this work lies even more in the fact that it furnishes so complete a picture of prevailing musical conditions in the neighboring areas of Liège and Avignon, and thus sets in bold relief the vital role Avignon played in shaping the music of the late Italian Ars Nova, where we find a mélange of the Italian and French styles.

————. "Propos sur l'Ars Nova." *RB* X (1956), 154–160.
This review of Fischer 32 seeks links with France and questions the validity of the term "Italian Ars Nova," since in Italy there had been no Ars Antiqua to precede it. Current Italian forms are related to chronology, yet it is emphasized that sharp dividing lines are impossible.

Corte, Andrea. *Le relazioni storiche della poesia e della musica italiana*. Torino, Pavia, 1936. Chapters I and II.

The Duecento is noted for its monody, as exemplified in the lauda, the monodic ballata, and the troubadour songs. To the credit of the Church, the religious songs (laude) have been preserved, enabling one to study their structure and thus to perceive the metric and spiritual relationships between words and music. On the other hand, since the layman paid little attention to secular monodic song, documentation regarding the monodic ballata remains scanty. This is largely true also of the troubadour songs, and as a consequence there is little proof of a suspected accompaniment on harp or viols. The spirit of the Italian Renaissance already makes itself felt in the pulsating humanism of the Trecento, and myriad poets contribute to Italy's superiority over France. Dante's *dolce stil nuovo* is equated with the Florentine Ars Nova, and both poetic and musical aspects of madrigal, caccia, and polyphonic ballata are discussed.

———— and G. Pannain. *Storia della musica.* Vol. I. Torino, 1944.
This work contributes nothing that has not been more thoroughly covered elsewhere but could prove useful to Italian readers. Sections deal with the lauda in Italy, monodic ballata ("Lucente stella," p. 142), polyphony in the fourteenth century, where "conductus and hocket reunite."

Culcasi, Carlo. *Il Petrarca e la musica.* Firenze, Bemporad, 1911.

D'Accone, Frank. "Le compagnie dei laudesi in Firenze durante l'Ars Nova." *Cert* III (1970), 253–280.

Damerini, Adelmo. "Introduzione al convegno . . . tenuto a Certaldo . . . , 1959." *Cert* I (1962), 3–17.
In introductory remarks addressed to the members of the first Certaldo Congress (1959), Adelmo Damerini paves the way for enlarging the sphere of studies, stressing the importance of Italy's role.

Davidsohn, R. *Firenze ai tempi di Dante.* Trans. by Eugenio D. Theseider. Firenze, R. Bemporad & Figlio, 1929.
A picture of the Florence of Dante. La poesia: 311–375; feste e divertimenti, musica, ballo a ginocchi: 503 ff.

Eggebrecht, Hans Heinrich. "Der Begriff des 'Neuen' in der Musik von der Ars Nova bis zur Gegenwart," *RIMS* (New York, 1961:1), 195–202.
The second of two papers read under the heading "The Concept of the 'New' in Music from the Ars Nova to the Present Day." Pages 196–198 apply to the Ars Nova, touching on the social climate of the period and the advocacy of the "old" *versus* the "new," as reflected respectively by Jacobus de Liège and John XXII, and by Johannes de Muris and Philippe de Vitry.

Einstein, Alfred. *The Italian Madrigal,* trans. by Oliver Strunk. Vol I. Princeton, N.J., Princeton University Press, 1949, 12–15.
The term "Ars Nova," even though applying primarily to the French movement, denotes not so much a new aesthetic content as a purely technical innovation. While the origins of the Italian Ars Nova must be sought in the French, nevertheless the former is no mere offshoot of the latter,

since it is characterized by strong distinguishing traits such as a more refined sense of form, a more sensuous tone quality, and an increased simplicity, all a part of the Florentine spirit. Music now claims equal rights
with poetry.

* Ellinwood, Leonard. "The Fourteenth Century in Italy." *NOH* (1960), 31–80.
This is a comprehensive résumé of the activity of a century in which "a
completely independent polyphonic art developed in Italy," and deals with
every aspect of this art: social background, extent of musical culture, music
in contemporary literature, influence of the poets, manuscript sources, notation, forms (including etymology of the term "madrigal"), composers,
thirteenth-century influence of the laudi spirituali and of the early Italian
trovatori who used the language and verse forms of Provence. It is stressed
that above all the principal source of the new Italian style is found in the
repertory of the conductus. Arguments are supported by numerous musical
examples.

————. "Francesco Landini and His Music." *MQ*, XXII (1936), 190–216.
This biographical sketch of Landini, with an exposition of his composi-
tional technique, stresses the importance of troubadour art in Italy, which
began with the crusades, when the Albigensian Crusade scattered troubadours from Provence. From the poet-singers the flame passed through Dante
to Petrarch, then to Sacchetti, with whom Landini was on intimate terms.[8]

————. "Origins of the Italian Ars Nova." *PAMS*, Dec. 1937, 29–37.
At the time this paper was read there was "only a handful of representative compositions . . . published in facsimile or in transcription." The
thesis is that the madrigal is derived from the conductus, but that there was
no transition through the motet. The myth invented by Burney(?) that
Casella set Dante to music is discredited, and Ludwig's reference to the
effect that "Casella diede il suono" is thought to be a quotation from a
Dante novella.[9]

————, ed. *The Works of Francesco Landini*. Cambridge, Mass., Mediaeval
Academy of America, 1939, xi–xlii.
More on Landini, his technique, and the milieu in which he wrote.

Fano, Fabio. "Origini della cappella musicale del duomo di Milano. Il primo
maestro di cappella: Matteo da Perugia (1402–16)." *RMI* LV (1953), 1–22.

————. *Le origini e il primo maestro di cappella: Matteo da Perugia*. Part I of
La Cappella musicale del duomo di Milano. Milano, Ricordi, 1956. (*IMAMI*,
nuova ser., 1.)
Some remarks on the period preceding the Ars Nova. A comparison between
the French and Italian Ars Nova, with particular reference to Matteo da
Perugia. Performance practices. Reviewed by Kurt von Fischer in *MF* XII
(1959), 223–230.

---

8. Wesselofsky.
9. *Ibid.* See also Bonaventura 2, 10–11, 131–132, as well as Pirrotta *14*, 653–654 and
Burney (op. cit.), 627–628. This would lead one to believe that Casella had indeed composed.

———. "Punti di vista su L'Ars Nova." *Cert* I (1962), 105–112.

A case is made for the application of the term "Ars Nova" to an entire century of activity by reason of the thread of continuity that runs from its inception to its end. In the final phase, the work of such men as Antonellus da Caserta and Ciconia demonstrates a reciprocity between the Italian and the French.

Fellerer, Gustav. "La 'Constitutio docta sanctorum patrum' di Giovanni XXII e la musica nuova del suo tempo." *Cert* I (1962), 9–17.

Regarding the problems posed by the appearance of secular polyphony as it threatened the music of the church, and regarding the efforts of John XXII to set limitations on it.

Fétis, François. *Histoire générale de la musique.* . . . Vol. V. Paris, Firmin-Didot, 1876, 307–313.

Ficker, Rudolf von. "Formprobleme der mittelalterlichen Musik." *ZfMW* VII (1924–25), 194–213.

The new music of Florence and of northern Italy displayed no link with the Gothic northern stream, for here the influence of Giotto and his followers can be felt. With the advent of secular music, individuality plays a major role, and the fetters of the northern motet school are absent. Melody is supreme, and melismas coming out of the East allow for a new melodic freedom. It is wrong to dismiss these as instrumental mannerism. Now there is a new concept of melody, and a union of melody, rhythm, and harmony.

———. "The Transition on the Continent." *NOH* (1960), 134–164.

Fischer, Kurt von. "Ars Nova." *EM* I (1963), 123–124.

Professor von Fischer now applies the term "Ars Nova" to both France and Italy [10] as denoting the new musical style of the fourteenth century, implemented by the new notation indicating note values and as set forth in the treatises of the period. The Papal Bull of 1324–25, and the general social milieu are considered. It is noteworthy that the small courts of Italy allow for more freedom, which generates a new element of improvised accompaniment, as well as embellished melody.

———. "Der Begriff des 'Neuen' in der Musik von der Ars Nova bis zur Gegenwart." *RIMS* (New York, 1961), 184–195.

This is the first of two papers read under the heading "The Concept of the 'New' in Music from the Ars Nova to the Present Day." The entire article is recommended, although pp. 189–190 apply specifically to the Ars Nova. In considering French *versus* Italian, it is emphasized that the new is in reality more significant in Italy, since unlike France, she had no polyphonic tradition. The paper follows the same line as that presented in the *Musical Quarterly* of January, 1961 (Fischer *20*), which is a revised and enlarged version of a paper read at the Certaldo Congress of 1959 (Fischer *6*). It is therefore recommended for German readers who cannot avail themselves of the other two papers mentioned here.

---

10. Perhaps here for pragmatic reasons?

* ———. "Les compositions à trois voix chez les compositeurs du Trecento."
Cert I (1962), 18–31.
An earlier and somewhat less comprehensive article than the one appearing
in the *Musical Quarterly* (Fischer 20). Recommended for French readers.

———. "Elementi arsnovistici nella musica boema antica." *Cert* II (1968), 77–83.
Regarding the influence of the Ars Nova abroad.

———. "G. Cesari–F. Fano: *La Cappella musicale del duomo di Milano. . . .*"
MF XII (1959), 223–230.
A review of the Fano work, with observations on Matteo da Perugia, on
Mod, and on the transition period, with its changes in notation style.

———. "Johannes Ciconia." *RB* XV (1961), 168–170.
An appraisal of the two-volume work on Ciconia by Suzanne Clercx, and a
reaffirmation of her conclusion that Ciconia is the principal exponent of
the Franco-Italian style so prominent at the end of the fourteenth century.
The relationship between Landini and Ciconia is considered, and there
are some remarks on the forms.

———. "Musica e società nel Trecento italiano." *Cert* III (1970), 11–28.
Every development initiated in the Duecento continued into the Trecento.
Some remarks on polyphony in Siena.

* ———. "On the Technique, Origin, and Evolution of Italian Trecento Music."
MQ XLVII:1 (Jan. 1961), 41–57.[11]
The Italian beginnings are seen in simple indigenous types of music making.
In challenging the varying theories of Ellinwood, Besseler, Pirrotta, and
other scholars regarding the derivation of the madrigal, the hypothesis is
advanced that the madrigal's structure seems to depend on an older instrumentally accompanied monody. In the course of its development
Trecento polyphony was influenced by the French style, even though the
Italian elements remained active. There follows an investigation into the
structure of two- and three-part Trecento compositions in relation to those
of the French Ars Nova, and observations are supported with musical
examples.

———. "Quelques remarques sur les relations entre les laudesi et les compositeurs florentins du Trecento." *Cert* III (1970), 247–252.
In Trecento Florence lauda singers and composers often shared equally in
social status. This close relationship leads to the hypothesis that in some
cases they may have been one and the same.

———. "Die Rolle der Mehrstimmingkeit am Dome von Siena zu Beginn des
13. Jahrhunderts." *AfMW* XVIII (1961), 167–182.
Some thoughts on polyphonic background.

* ———. *Studien zur italienischen Musik des Trecento und frühen Quattrocento.*
Bern, Haupt, 1956. (Publikationen der Schweizerischen musikforschenden
Gesellschaft, Ser. 2, Vol. V.)

---

11. See also Fischer *4*.

An invaluable and comprehensive inventory of the musical output of this period (confined to madrigali, cacce, and ballate), arranged by form, then by text incipit. Tables indicate poet, composer, number of voices, manuscript sources, transcriptions, and facsimile editions. Separate sections on composers, poets, sources, notation, concordances. Particularly useful is the extensive section on notation. The composer index with tables indicates the total output of each, proportional occurrence in the manuscripts, etc. The Introduction deals with recent musical researches and with disputed points. Reviewed by Clercx in *RB* X (1956), 154–160, who recognizes a scrupulous observance of documents but objects to the use of too many symbols, and by Reaney in *ML* XXXVII (1956), 392–394, who generally approves, though he would prefer a more extensive literary bibliography. He also deplores the use of percentages and questions some of Fischer's attributions. Discussions on three aspects of *Studien* . . . took place at the Colloques de Wégimont, 1955, and are published in *Wég* (1959), 27–34, 131–136, 232–238.

* ———. "Trecentomusik–Trecentoprobleme." *Acta* XXX (1958), 179–199.
This is for the most part a survey of the achievements of over half a century of scholarly research, which have resulted in (1) the appearance of a number of monuments in transcription, (2) new discoveries of sources, (3) a closer approximation of manuscript chronology, (4) more biographical data. We now have a clearer picture of the beginnings of the Trecento as well as of the transition into the Quattrocento. But there remain the perennial questions of "Trecento" *versus* "Ars Nova" and of the extent of French influence.

Frati, Ludovico. "Il Petrarca e la musica." *RMI* XXXI (1924), 59–68.

* Gandolfi, Riccardo. *Illustrazioni d'alcuni cimeli concernenti l'arte musicale in Firenze,* Firenze, La Commissione per l'esposizione di Vienna, 1892. 28 pp. (29 leaves), 39 plates.
Possibly the earliest monograph devoted to the subject under consideration, with 39 plates containing facsimiles of one-, two-, and three-voiced compositions, portraits of composers, and a brief description and history of the Squarcialupi Codex. Introduction (pp. 13–18) deals with the important role of Florence—and of Giotto, Dante, and Landini in particular—with reference to traits typical of Italy's melody making.

Gasperini, Guido. "L'art musical italien au XIVᵉ siècle." *EC* I:2 (1913), 611–619.
The element of spontaneity is stressed, with the conviction that there is no tradition other than that from Provence. Reference is made to "La petite musique italienne du XIVᵐᵉ siècle." The principal emphasis is on the theorists and the development of mensural notation and of the new rhythmic variety resulting from it.

Ghisi, Federico. "An Angel Concert in a Trecento Sienese Fresco." *ReeFest* (1966), 308–313.
This article and the following one shed some light on social life in Trecento Tuscany, with particular respect to musical performance.

————. "Angeli musicanti in una tavola attribuita al Giottino nel museo del Bargello di Firenze." *Cert* II (1968), 91–96.

————. "Danza e strumenti nella pittura senese del Trecento." *Cert* III (1970), 83–104.

————. "La persistance du sentiment monodique et l'évolution de la polyphonie italienne du XIVᵉ au XVᵉ siècle." *Wég* (1959), 217–231.

> The evolution of Italian polyphony in the fourteenth and fifteenth centuries is demonstrated by means of a polyphonic lauda of Jacopo which, when rewritten without the vocal melismas, approaches the fifteenth-century style.

————. "Rapporti armonici nella polifonia italiana del Trecento." *Cert* I (1962), 32–39.

> By means of documentation, it is demonstrated that some harmonic relations in Italian Trecento music are derived from medieval polyphony and from the French Ars Nova. Author stresses the importance of *hearing* the music of each period in order to relate it, step by step, to the succeeding ones. Special reference to Zachara da Teramo, Andrea dei Servi, and Egidio and Guglielmo di Francia.

Gombosi, Otto. "French Secular Music of the Fourteenth Century." *MQ* XXXVI (1950), 603–610.

> A review of Apel *1*. Deals with French influence on Italy—that is, French composers writing in the Italian style and vice versa.

Günther, Ursula. "Les Colloques de Wégimont." *MF* XIV (1961), 210–213.

> A review of the papers read at the Colloques de Wégimont, 1955, and published in 1959.

————. "Das Ende der Ars Nova." *MF* XVI (1963), 105–120.[12]

> The reader who seeks enlightenment on the varying concepts and applications of the term "late Ars Nova" can do no better than to commence his investigations with this very scholarly and relevant study, although the remarks are for the greater part directed toward the French school. The problem is approached with respect to chronology and style, the two elements that dictate terminology; and the varying interpretations of scholars working in this area have been assembled in concise yet thorough form. *The question is not when the Ars Nova begins but rather when it ends,* and the argument here presented is that the emergence of the *ars subtilior* spells the demise of the Ars Nova.
>
> In the latter part of the fourteenth century there is a reciprocal influence between France and Italy, and a new style emerges that is characterized by a wider and more complex variety of rhythms and notation. The question is raised regarding the validity of the expression "late Ars Nova," a term that has enjoyed wide usage in denoting the musical activity of this period. Two alternative terms are considered. Apel *1* calls the notation "mannered notation" and writes of the "manneristic period." The varying

---

12. This issue of *MF* arrived at the University of California Library *after* the first edition of this guide had gone to the press.

and subtle implications of the term "mannerism" are weighed, and the question is put whether it is applicable here. An analysis of Guido's ballade, "Or voit tout en aventure," appropriately sheds new light on the end of the Ars Nova epoch, and lends some validity to the term "mannerism," for in the text, doubtless also written by the composer,[13] we find "Nos faysoms contre nature. . . ."

Ars subtilior is looked on with favor, for it is pointed out that subtilior is the comparative of subtilis or subtilitas. The former was used early in the century by Jacobus de Liège and somewhat later by other theorists. Pirrotta *15* speaks of "subtilitas" in referring to the polyphonic practice of the early fourteenth century. When did the change from Ars Nova or *ars subtilis* to *ars subtilior* take place? At the onset of the more complicated style, i.e., 1370–1377, according to various scholars. There is an unquestioned parallel between the schism (1378–1417) and this new direction. By the 1380s the new style was widely disseminated, although Landini remained relatively untouched by it. Nowhere is this *ars subtilior* better exemplified than in the works of Matteo da Perugia, but it extends even as far as Dufay.

———. "Die Mensuralnotation der Ars Nova in Theorie und Praxis." *AfMW* XIX–XX:1 (1962–63), 9–28.

The objective is to demonstrate the practice of mensural notation by means of the compositions themselves, since they are more reliable and convincing than theoretical treatises. The positions taken by Borren and Wolf that Italy must have introduced the binaria into France are held as untenable; and it is agreed with Besseler, Handschin, and Reaney that in France there had been evidence of duple rhythms even before the fourteenth century. The former theory is discredited by means of examples demonstrating that the superiority of the French system led to a more rapid development of the new complicated rhythms, and the conclusion is that the Italian influence is negligible, if not entirely nonexistent. There is a listing of the most important factors in this investigation which lead to the above stated conclusion.

Gutmann, Hans. "Der Decamerone des Boccaccio als musikgeschichtliche Quelle." *ZfMW* XI (1928–29), 397–401.

Handschin, Jacques. *Musikgeschichte im Überblick*. Lucerne, Räber & Cie, 1948, 197–209.

There were no musical monuments in Italy in the second half of the thirteenth century, though Villani speaks of the music in the Duomo of Florence. Is there justification for the term "Neue Kunst" to be applied to both France and Italy when what we are dealing with in the first half of the fourteenth century is not *new music* but a *new method* of [mensural] notation, which is here described? As a result, rhythm is now freed from its former limitations. The vocal polyphonic art now flourishing in Italy displays the characteristic Italian melodic curve and smoothness of rhythm. Madrigal is likened to conductus and ballata to virelai.

---

13. *Fl.* 1380 (*MGG* V, 1078–1079).

————. "Die Rolle der Nationen in der Musikgeschichte." *SJfMW* V (1931), 25–42.

> An overall picture, with a consideration of the literal *versus* the broader concept of Ars Nova and of the differing style elements. Observations on the madrigal, its roots, etymology of the word, etc. Footnotes in this article are of the utmost importance.

Harman, Alec. *Mediaeval and Early Renaissance Music*. London, Rockliff, 1958, 153–173.

> The reader is advised to study the entire chapter on "The New Art" (pp. 121–184) before proceeding to the discussion of the Italian Ars Nova. This takes into account the strong influence of France, yet stresses the unique characteristics of the Italian art of the period, namely, a conspicuous presence of melody and color, and the use of imitation. There is one musical example for each of the three forms: madrigal, caccia, and ballata. Italian notation is also considered.

Harrison, Frank. "Tradition and Innovation in Instrumental Usage, 1100–1450." *ReeFest* (1966), 319–335.

> In the continuing culture of late antiquity there was presumably a wide popular demand for the laudi of *joculatores Dei* to be written down in the vernacular in order to implement the evangelical work of the Franciscans. "Marchettus' *Pomerium* of 1318" was written for the professionals who catered to the well-to-do citizenry. In this treatise Marchettus contrasts the French methods with his own.

Königslöw, Annamarie von. *Die italienischen Madrigalisten des Trecento*. Würzburg, Triltsch, 1940.

> Background. Metrical forms and their musical application. Composers, divided into early and middle periods, peak, and decline. Musical examples. **Bibliography.**

Korte, Werner. *Studien zur Geschichte der Musik in Italien im ersten Viertel des 15. Jahrhunderts*. Kassel, Bärenreiter, 1933.

> Particularly helpful in identifying some composers, and in placing them chronologically and geographically.

* LiGotti, Ettore. *La poesia musicale italiana del secolo XIV*. Palermo, Palumbo, 1944.

> The title of this compact work is misleading, for it actually deals with many aspects of Italian Trecento music. It is unique in its subjective and unusually sensitive approach to the composers and to their music, and it is an invaluable aid in appraising the activity of this period.

* ————. *Restauri trecenteschi*. Palermo, Palumbo, 1947.

> A collection of essays dealing with a variety of subjects, each linked to the literary background of Trecento music.

Liuzzi, Fernando. *La lauda e i primordi della melodia italiana*. Vol. I. Roma, Libreria dello Stato, 1935.

> This is a documentation of the history of Italian melody during the decades

preceding the Ars Nova, from St. Francis to Dante, when the lauda becomes the spiritual sister of the monodic ballata. With the Franciscans there
emerge the oldest know experiments with popular religious lyric poetry.
Those attributes common to both lauda and ballata at the end of the
thirteenth and beginning of the fourteenth centuries are a sincerity and
simplicity of language which reflect contemporary customs. The ballata, after
its first flowering, becomes elastic and varied. The reader is advised to consult the bibliography, pp. 21–24.

————. "Le relazioni musicali tra Fiandra e Italia nel secolo XV." *Institut
historique belge de Rome,* Bull. XIX (1938), 189–203.
   Deals principally with later fifteenth century but contains some remarks on
   the first decades and on some composers and sources of the period.

Ludwig, Friedrich. "Geschichte der Mensural-Notation von 1250–1460." *SIMG* VI
(1904–05), 597–641.
   A lengthy and critical review of Wolf 5, in which are enumerated areas of
   disagreement, namely, that Florence was not the only center, that Padua
   was not within the sphere of Florentine influence, that Italian history of
   this period was divided into central (specially Florence) and northern. Wolf
   disregards Ludwig's previous observations regarding the four leading
   manuscripts (two in Florence and two in Paris) and their chronology. The
   former commences his description with the largest and *latest,* Sq, seeming
   to overlook the varying forms of notation in other manuscripts. Included
   are lists of composers in chronological sequence and of the sources then
   known.

* ————. "Italienische Madrigale, Balladen und Cacce." In *Handbuch der
Musikgeschichte,* ed. by Guido Adler. 2d ed. Vol. I. Berlin, M. Hess, 1930,
277–291.

* ————. "Die mehrstimmige Musik des 14. Jahrhunderts." *SIMG* IV (1902–03),
16–69.
   This article underscores the importance of understanding the liturgical and
   sacred background before studying the development of fourteenth-century
   polyphony. In contrasting the new Italian school with the French, the
   individuality of the Italian compositions is stressed. The practice of writing
   a free melisma in one voice, unknown to the French, proves shocking to
   contemporaries, yet carries with it an indebtedness to Italy for introducing
   the coloratura element into vocal music. Landini, taking his texts from
   the treasures of Italian poetry, is to Italy what Machaut is to France.
   Sources (five major and numerous minor ones) are listed, as are the names
   of some two dozen composers who produced about five hundred works,
   one-third of which were to Landini's credit.

* Marrocco. "Integrated Devices in the Music of the Italian Trecento." *Cert*
III (1970), 411–429.
   Eight integrative devices are discussed briefly and illustrated with examples. These are partial imitation, pervading motive, variation, ostinato,
   isorhythm, dialogue, homorhythm, and equal participation. There are also

some observations on Italo-Gallic intercourse, and the paper concludes with
the reminder that the remarkably florid art of bel canto of this period,
while most certainly bearing the stamp of individuality, at the same time
displays evidence of having assimilated and utilized devices and artifices
from northern neighbors. Nevertheless, Italy did not surrender her national identity. Documentary footnotes are most valuable.

Martinez-Göllner, Marie Louise. "L'Ars Nova italiana del Trecento. . . ." *MF*
XVII (1964), 432–433.
 A review of the Certaldo conference in 1959. Abstracts of Pirrotta *35*,
Fischer *6*, Seay *3*, and others.

*————. *Die Musik des frühen Trecento*. Tutzing, 1963 (*Münchener Ver-
öffentlichungen zur Musikgeschichte, 9*).
 An examination of the theoretical treatises now at our disposal, together
with the earliest two-voiced madrigals of Rs, reveals no evidence of a
preexisting tenor and leads to the conclusion that, unlike French works
of this period, Trecento polyphony had its origins in the Italian monodic
tradition.[14] Yet in view of the spotty musical tradition in Italy before 1300,
it is felt that this singular type of musical composition cannot stand as an
isolated phenomenon, and that a connection with France is not to be dis-
missed.[15] The nature and development of madrigal, caccia and ballata are
discussed, together with the divergent opinions of scholars regarding them.
French notations is contrasted with Italian, and an analysis of the work of
Marchettus brings into sharp focus his raised leading tone (not without
allowing credits to previous studies in this area).[16] Diagrams of the first
five madrigals of Rs demonstrate a familiarity with a tonal center. This
cogent and well-documented piece of writing also contains some pertinent
remarks on performance practice, and there are facsimiles of twelve works.
The brief selective bibliography is useful, but even more so are the documentary footnotes.

Meyer-Baer, Kathi. "Music in Dante's *Divina commedia*." *ReeFest* (1966), 614–
627.
 The *Commedia* reflects all facets of the culture of its time and also reveals
the music-making practice of the period. Casella is the only musician mentioned in this work, and the author of this article speculates that perhaps
Dante and Casella wrote both music and poetry in their youth.[17] The
canzone belongs to the *dolce stil nuovo*, a term formulated by Dante in
the Purgatorio. This new style, or Ars Nova, was the result of the linking
of the art of the Provençal troubadours with the different schools of Italian
poetry.

Nolthenius, Hélène. *In that Dawn*. London, Longman & Todd, 1968.
 Useful for background dealing with the culture of the Duecento, the laude,
etc. Consult also bibliographies for each chapter.

---

14. In disagreement with Ludwig *4*, 60; Besseler *11*, 157; Ellinwood *3*, 29. In agreement with Liuzzi *2*, 40 ff; Ghisi *12*, 217 ff; Fischer *20*, 41, 47.
 15. Examples of such connections in the early fourteenth century are cited on p. 131.
 16. Ludwig *4*, 62; Besseler *11*, 159; Ficker *1*, 209; Pirrotta *34*:II, 139; Marrocco *7*, 24.
 17. See also WolfSq, Introduction. For more on Casella, see n. 9, above.

OH I (1929), 269–296.
   Musica ficta, pp. 269–279; the papal bull (1324–25), in Latin and English,
   pp. 294–296.

* Perroy, Edouard. "Le point de vue de l'historien." *Wég* (1959), 261–269.
   A historian views the Ars Nova in the sociopolitical perspective of the
   fourteenth century, which he sees as one of the great centuries in a long
   and changing period. With reference to France and Italy, it is closely
   linked with the search to free oneself from the shackles of the preceding
   century. The many aspects of the economic revolution are cited as part
   of the social reform, or "style nouveau," which manifested itself also in art
   and music. As a result, despite the opposition of the Church, the *via
   moderna,* in replacing the *via antiqua,* becomes more than a musical style.

Perz, Miroslaw. "Die Einflüsse der ausgehenden italienischen Ars Nova in
   Polen." *Cert* III (1970), 465–483.
   Regarding influence abroad.

* Pirrotta, Nino. "Ars Nova." *Musica* I:1 (1966), 189–197.
   Comprehensive coverage is compressed into these few pages. A summation
   of the continuing polemic surrounding terminology concludes that the
   term Ars Nova should not be restricted to its original Latin connotation,
   but that it is more applicable to an artistic conception. There follow considerations of the treatises of Petrus de Cruce, Johannes de Muris, Vitry,
   Marchettus, and Jacobus de Liège and a reemphasis of the meteoric rise
   of Italy. Before and immediately following this Italian Ars Nova period
   the predominantly monodic forms presented little need for a complicated
   notation. Relative to the early years of the Trecento, neither in Antonio da
   Tempo's treatise (*Delle rime volgari,* 1332) nor in Rs is there any distinc-
   tion in the poetic forms between those destined for monodic versus polyphonic treatment. Page 195 deals with some specifics of the later period,
   such as Florence in particular, Landini and the polyphonic ballata, and
   mannerism, that tendency toward artificiality which manifested itself at the
   end of the century. See also bibliography.

* ———. "Ars Nova e stil novo." *RIM* I:1 (1966), 3–19.
   The Italian version of a paper read at the Dante Symposium at Johns
   Hopkins, 1965, in which Dr. Pirrotta, having first posed the question
   whether there is justification for introducing the Ars Nova into a Dante
   celebration, now considers the possibility of a connection and states his
   reasons for so doing, namely, that this meteoric outburst of polyphonic
   activity took place in a century that had been inaugurated by Dante and
   Giotto and that was resolved by the voices of Petrarch and Boccaccio. The
   characteristics of the *stil novo* abound in the Ars Nova output; and Riemann, in referring to Florence as the cradle of the Ars Nova, evidently
   relates it to the *dolce stil novo.* Yet the years immediately preceding 1330
   seemed unimportant to Riemann. The fact is that all references to music
   of that period were made not to polyphonic activity, but rather to the
   various genres of the unwritten, from the troubadour type of street song
   to the dance music and to the religious lauda. In this latter case the music

remained religious but was now used for secular texts. The ballata in its earliest monodic form is the principal vehicle of the musical expression of the *stil novo* and by the same token is the oldest. Only later does it become polyphonic (*ca.* 1370), when it is written with such enthusiasm that madrigal and caccia fall into disuse. Most of the manuscripts from Florence correspond in time and place with the current ideas of Dante's "poesia volgare," and there is a link between the creative impulse of the *stil novo* and the increased polyphonic activity of the Ars Nova. In at least one case the dependence of medieval culture on France is broken, thanks to Dante. The merit of the Italian Ars Nova is found in its own unique style of refined equilibrium and freshness of expression. In stressing the separation between written and unwritten music, the author points out with Torrefranca that the unlocked "secret" of the mid-Quattrocento, somewhat paralleling that of the pre-Ars Nova period, may be ascribed to a reverting reliance on the unwritten.

―――. "Cronologia e denominazione dell'Ars Nova italiana." *Wég* (1959), 93–109.
A consideration of the difficulties encountered in establishing chronology, because without exception the manuscripts were compiled some 20 to 30 years after actual composition. A challenge to Besseler's literal and more narrow interpretation of Ars Nova.

―――. "Dulcedo e subtilitas nella pratica polifonica franco-italiana al principio del '400." *RB* II:3–4 (1948), 125–132.
Dulcedo and *subtilitas* were in reality opposite poles. The latter offered the widest range of possibilities, and the theories on which fourteenth-century music was based were superseded by a myriad of new writing, of which the Modena Codex in particular is an example. The introduction of French stylistic and technical elements into Italian polyphony at the turn of the century has all the characteristics of yet another phenomenon, that of a change in musical taste.

―――. "Italien. B) 14–16 Jahrhundert." *MGG* VI (1957), 1476–1480.

―――. "Lirica monodica trecentesca." *RaM* IX (1936), 317–325.
This calls attention to the "monodic intonations" that were found among the polyphonic ones, chiefly in the codices Sq and Rs, and that were composed principally by Lorenzo and Gherardello. Musical examples.

* ―――. "Il madrigale e la caccia." *CorteA* (1945), 57–61.
This is an aesthetic approach to the entire question, and the spirit of the cultural world in Italy is contrasted with that of France. Whereas in France an intellectual posture predominates, in Italy composers rely more on their intuition. Some consideration is given to the structure of the madrigal and of the canonic madrigal, which closely resembles the caccia.

* ―――. "Marchettus de Padua and the Italian Ars Nova." *MD* IX (1955), 51–71.
An investigation of the conditions surrounding the birth of the Italian Ars

Nova, relating the *Lucidarium* and the *Pomerium* to them. Additional documentation lends support to Strunk's conclusions that the *Pomerium* dates from about 1319 and, thus, would explode the hypothesis that Marchettus was influenced by Vitry and by Johannes de Muris. The conclusion negates the theories that France was responsible for the Italian system of rhythmic notation and that France influenced early Italian chromaticism. The period before the "first generation" and the Florentine period is discussed, and other regions of activity are considered.

———, ed. *The Music of Fourteenth-Century Italy*. Rome, American Institute of Musicology, 1954–1963. Forewords to all volumes.

* ——— and LiGotti. *Il Sacchetti e la tecnica musicale del Trecento italiano*. Firenze, G. C. Sansoni, 1935. With musical supplement.

Two scholars, one literary, the other musical, approach this subject from their respective points of view: "Tecnica poetica," by LiGotti; "Pratica e tecnica musicale," by Pirrotta. The latter section deals principally with the relationship between music and poetry. This relationship can be reduced to three fundamental patterns: music and poetry, being of equal importance, are adapted one to the other; music is subservient to poetry; poetry bows to music. Up to the end of the Duecento and the beginning of the Trecento (through the Dante period), patterns one and two prevail exclusively. The same music is sometimes even used for both sacred and secular texts, as with the laude (and monodic ballate). In the Trecento, pattern three appears, and we have "poesia per musica." With this there is a refinement of rhythms through mensural notation, and the development of a contrapuntal technic brings with it new possibilities. As new demands are made on singers, the "cantori specializzati" appear on the scene. The three forms—madrigal, caccia, and polyphonic ballata—are discussed, as well as the etymology of the word "madrigal." See p. 50 for the monodic ballata. Footnotes serve as a bibliography and also abound in information that is as pertinent as that contained in the body of the text. For example, p. 62 n. 3: "The affirmation that the Italian Ars Nova is exclusively secular . . . appears too uncompromising. . . ." The motets *Lux purpurata* and *Gratiosus magnanissimus* are cited as examples. Despite the fact that this work was written thirty-five years ago, it remains one of the most important studies in the field.

———. "Tradizione orale e tradizione scritta della musica." *Cert* III (1970), 431–439.

A reiteration of views expressed earlier (Pirrotta 3) regarding written tradition vis à vis oral tradition in music. These remarks are directed more to a later period.

* Reaney, Gilbert. "Ars Nova." In *Pelican History of Music*, Vol. I, ed. by A. Robertson and Denis Stevens. Penguin Books, 1960, 261–308.

This work is of particular value to the student who is not proficient in foreign languages and can take its place beside the two chapters in the *New Oxford History* as providing the most comprehensive English language coverage of the secular musical activity of this century (Fischer *20* is also most useful for Italy). Pages 291–308 deal specifically with Italy; nevertheless, the significance of this movement cannot be thoroughly grasped without a careful perusal of the preceding thirty pages, which provide a concise survey of the historical and cultural background. Here again is a consideration of the label "Ars Nova," a label that is stylistic in its connotation. Italy is compared with France. Whereas the Gothic style of the latter soars, the former is more earthbound. In France there were the continued chivalric *romans;* in Italy, such masterpieces as Dante's *Commedia* and Boccaccio's *Decamerone.* Vitry's *Ars Nova* is considered vis à vis Marchettus' *Pomerium,* and the importance of Petrus de Cruce is underscored. Italian notation is more adaptable to the coloratura style of the Italian, as opposed to the more frequent use of the hocket in the French. There follows a study of the forms and of some important composers. Late in the fourteenth century the Italian style incorporates some French features, though the use of French texts is relatively rare.

———. "The Middle Ages." In *A History of Song,* ed. by Denis Stevens, 2d ed. New York, Norton, 1970, 37–62.
Cogent remarks on the Trecento's debt to the monodic lauda and to the conductus. Also observations on performance practice and on the principal composers and their respective styles.

———. "Studien zur italienischen Musik des Trecento und frühen Quattrocento. . . ." *ML* XXXVII (1956), 392–394.
A review of Fischer's *Studien.* . . .

* Reese, Gustave. *Music in the Middle Ages.* New York, W. W. Norton, 1940.
Chapter 11 (p. 294) is recommended for background reading, since it deals with the great Gothic polyphony of the Notre Dame school (twelfth and thirteenth centuries). Chapter 12 concerns itself with fourteenth-century France and p. 340 with the still unresolved question regarding chronological priority of Vitry's *Ars Nova* versus Marchettus' *Pomerium.* Chapter 13 begins with a recognition of the nonliturgical monody of the Duecento lauda, and the unique contributions of Italy are enumerated, namely, that she produced a body of fresh polyphony in which the melisma played an important role; that whereas the main melody of the conductus had usually been in the lower voice, it is now shifted to the top. Italy now becomes divorced from the cantus firmus, and there is an early "feeling for tonality." Trecento composers are listed by generation, following Ellinwood's arrangement. The view on performance practice tends to be that, since this art is *Kunstlied,* the melismas might well be intended for the voice.

———. *Music in the Renaissance.* Rev. ed. New York, Norton, 1959, 24–33.

Riemann, Hugo. "Florenz, die Wiege der Ars Nova." Riemann *2,* I:2 (1905), 297–335.
The first to apply the term "Ars Nova" to Italy, Riemann held the view that the phenomenon of Italy has been underrated, that it is not connected with the Paris school, and that if one must seek an outside influence it can

but come from Provençal troubadour poetry. The instrumental accompaniment of these troubadour songs is based on the principle of accompanied
monody, and the melismas, occurring particularly at the beginning and
at the end, are very likely instrumental executions.

————. "Das Kunstlied im 14.–15." Jahrhundert." *SIMG* VII (1905–6), 529–550.
Dr. Riemann's outlook on the Ars Nova period is more unique than that
of his colleagues, for he prefers to look on this activity as a new art song
brought about by a change of mood, rather than as a set of technical and
mechanical innovations, obviously made possible by the new notation. To
support his thesis he cites examples from the "tone painters" Paolo and
Piero. His emphasis is more on actual practice than on theory. Here again
the case is stated for instrumental accompaniment and for the instrumental
execution of the opening and ending melismas, citing a reference to this
in the *Decamerone*. A tenable hypothesis is advanced that perhaps in the
end the custom of accompanying songs on the lute had passed from Spain
to Italy.

Sachs, Kurt. *Rhythm and Tempo: A Study in Music History.* New York, 1953,
179–197.
Fourteenth-century France is contrasted with Trecento Italy. The former
did not experience a change in the musical concept, and the Gothic was
more concerned with "musical engineering" than with musical imagina-
tion. In Italy, on the contrary, the climate was more revolutionary. Here
was a new world of poets and color. In her preference for time signatures
she also differed from her northern neighbor, for she favored the use of
imperfection, or the binary, to an extent not found in France.

Schering, Arnold. " 'Ars antiqua' e 'ars nova.' " CorteA (1945), 42–46.
In contrasting the Ars Antiqua with the Ars Nova, a study of the music
itself is favored over a study of the theory. The *Speculum*, then thought to
be by Johannes de Muris but now known to be by Jacobus de Liège, is
considered the most revealing of the then contemporary theoretical writings. The author of this treatise revolted against the "modern rude . . .
and ignorant "cantores' " (here *cantores* means anyone who makes music)
who held in contempt the old, which they thought had neither the *subtilitas* nor the complicated structure of the new. Important role of the
organ is stressed.

* ————. *Studien zur Musikgeschichte der Frührenaissance.* Leipzig, C. F. Kant
Nachfolger, 1914.
In the introduction and early pages of this masterly study [18] it is emphasized that the new cannot be divorced from what came before, and that
one must give the Ars Antiqua its due investigation. It is for this reason
that the reader is advised to study at least the first 123 pages of this
work. The bridge between the old and the new is not to be found in
speculative theory, but in the living practice of the art, and a plea is
made for placing periods in their proper perspective. Unlike Riemann, who

18. Restricted though the resources were.

feels that the Ars Nova came into being in 1334–1342, this author believes that it was already coming to life two decades earlier, with the dying Ars Antiqua, and that it was the triumph of the new instrumentally accompanied song that actually ushered in the new. With this came the resistance of the Church. In citing a parallel between Paumann's organ arrangement of "Des klaffers neyden" and Giovanni's "Nascoso il viso," the question is posed whether these resemblances may not indeed go deeper, particularly since Giovanni himself was an organist (pp. 16–17). We are reminded that the greater part of Paumann's compositions are arrangements of folk melodies. In this connection much consideration is given to the positive and the portative organs of Landini's time and to him and his image as an organist. Schering's thesis in all of his writings remains the same, namely that these melodies were not only accompanied by the organ, but that they were often played in entirety by it and other instruments, such as the lute and viola (as illustrated in Gandolfi 2).

Schneider, Marius. *Die Ars Nova des XIV Jahrhunderts in Frankreich und Italien.* Wolfenbüttel-Berlin, Kallmeyer, 1930.
More emphasis and space devoted to French, but with some comparisons between French and Italian.

———. "Das gestalttypologische Verfahren in der Melodik des Francesco Landino." *Acta* XXXV (1963), 2–14.
An analysis of three compositions of Landini demonstrates his use of the eastern Gestalt technique and the connection between the Italian Ars Nova and Incid-Mediterranean music making. Could not this perhaps account for the melismas that abound in Italian Ars Nova compositions?

———. "Klagelieder des Volkes in der Kunstmusik der italienischen Ars Nova." *Acta* XXXIII (1961), 162–168.
The character of the Sicilian and Corsican folk lament is displayed in examples from Landini and Andrea (as particularly related to the Mediterranean melisma), with the conclusion that a closer examination of the Italian compositions of this period reveals in reality many more of the older elements than would appear on the surface. It is because the technique of the Ars Nova is to a large extent controlled by structural laws that these older elements are not readily detected, and a strong plea is made for further research into this area.

Schrade, Leo. "The Chronology of the Ars Nova in France." *Wég* (1959), 32–62.
Deals with terminology as well as with chronology in both Italy and France.

———, ed. *The Works of Francesco Landini.* Monaco, Editions de l'Oiseau-Lyre, 1958 (*PMF,* 4). Commentary.
Italian Trecento music lends itself to a more easy and natural understanding than the French, which is rationalistically organized and tends to be contrived. Regarding the studies of Ludwig and Wolf, the former inclines more toward the roots of the music and its interpretation, whereas the latter is more interested in the theory.

Seay, Albert. *Music in the Medieval World.* Englewood Cliffs, N.J., Prentice-Hall, 1965.[19]
>A good English language coverage. Again it is recommended that the student study the entire work. Pages 149–166 deal with a comparison between French and Italian art, forms, chronology, geographical distribution, and composers (particularly Landini), and contain fragments of musical examples. Bibliography is very brief.

Smith, F. Joseph. "Ars Nova—a Redefinition?" *MD* XVIII (1964), 19–35; XIX (1965), 83–97.
>This article represents a unique stance in the ever-present Ars Nova polemic. Likening this term to that of the twentieth-century *Neue Musik*, it is asked whether this too is not a mere slogan imposed by historiographers. The Ars Nova, in planting the seed that disrupted the rationality of the Middle Ages, dealt a death blow to the medieval age of reason. It therefore follows that in order to redefine Ars Nova we must again study the rational background of the medieval theory of the Ars Antiqua, with its mathematical concepts of sound, number, and proportion. Particularly important is the concept of number, for consonance is represented by the sacred number three and is disrupted by the new dissonance. Jacobus de Liège remains the champion of the rational consonance in medieval music theory; and a reediting and reevaluation of the *Speculum* is recommended, for this treatise is considered to be the key to understanding the true significance of this historic upheaval. For this reevaluation (1966), see the section on theory (VII), p. 73, below.

Strunk, Oliver. "Intorno a Marchetto da Padova." *RaM* XX (1950), 312–315.
>Marchettus is the principal spokesman of the Trecento through his *Lucidarium* (plainsong) and *Pomerium* (mensural notation). In setting out to establish the date of the *Pomerium* vis à vis the treatises of Vitry and Johannes de Muris, the varying hypotheses of earlier scholars are first weighed. By relating its appearance to historical facts, it is here concluded that it was written no later than April 1319, and therefore the first Trecentists were in no way dependent on Johannes de Muris or Vitry.[20]

Vecchi, Giuseppe. "Letteratura e musica nel Trecento." *Cert* III (1970), 485–503.
>All literary and documentary allusions to the Duecento and Trecento depict a society dedicated to pleasing songs and pleasing sounds ("canti e suoni").

———. "Teorie e prassi nel canto a due voci in Italia nel Duecento e nel primo Trecento." *Cert* III (1970), 203–214.
>In considering theory *versus* practice, it is the latter, enhanced by harmo-

---

19. Announced by Arno Volk Verlag (Köln) for late 1971; Seay, "Das 14. Jahrhundert: Ars Nova und Trecento," *Die Mehrstimmige Musik des Mittelalters bis zum Ausgang des 15. Jahrhunderts (Palaeographie der Musik, 2).*
20. More on this in the section on theory (VII), p. 69, below.

nious intuition and innate lyrical resources, that imparts to this Italian art a sense of modernity and freshness.

―――. "Tra monodia e polifonia." *CHM* II (1957), 447–464.

Deals principally with sacred music, but its concern with the lauda renders it relevant. It is felt that the Duecento has not yet been seen in its totality, and this article represents an investigation into the slow maturation of the musical experiments of this century, without which the astonishing achievements of the Trecento could not have been accomplished. The young lauda is considered hand in hand with a mature hymnody, where monody find a place by the side of polyphony and the vernacular a place beside the Latin. It is not enough to limit one's observations to the lauda output. One should rather recognize the Duecento as a century of faith, when the brotherhoods inject a brighter profession of faith into the song and language of the people. Soon the monodic ballata imposes itself on the lauda.

Wesselofsky, Alessandro, ed. *"Il paradiso degli Alberti" di Giovanni da Prato.* 3 vols. Bologna, Romagnoli, 1867.

Giovanni da Prato's novel, *Il paradiso degli Alberti,* written about 1390, deals with life in Florence, including its musical aspects. This work is in many ways more revealing than the *Decamerone,* since in this case the characters are real, not fictional.

White, John Reeves. "Music of the Early Italian Ars Nova." 2 vols. Unpublished doctoral dissertation, University of Indiana, 1952.

Wolf, Johannes. "Firenze musicale nel '300." CorteA (1945), 46–50.

This is not as comprehensive as the following citation, but useful for one not reading German.

* ―――. "Florenz in der Musikgeschichte des 14. Jahrhunderts." *SIMG* III (1901–02), 599–646.

One of the earliest pioneer studies on Trecento Florence,[21] and for this reason alone it must always remain in every bibliography relating to this period. In surveying briefly the rich French background, it is conceded that in Italy there was little musical activity between the years of Guido and the mid-thirteenth century. There was no Lied literature in Italy, and northern Italy took delight in Provençal poetry. About the middle of the Duecento Italy developed its own vernacular poetry, and during the Dante period Florence was a rich and flourishing city. Poets were no doubt also composers, as Casella may have been (p. 600), and perhaps the same was true of Dante. Florentine musical activity begins early in the fourteenth century, and the notation practice of that time is described in the *Pomerium,* "soon after 1309." Sources, composers, poets, and distinguishing characteristics are enumerated. Musical supplement.

* ―――. *Geschichte der Mensural-Notation von 1250–1460.* 3 vols. Leipzig, Breitkopf & Härtel, 1904.

―――――――――――

21. Brief articles had been written earlier. See n. 4.

Wolf here "blazed his now well-known trail into the Italian Trecento repertoire" [22] by providing the key to the secret of mensural notation. Each stage is analyzed with profuse musical examples. Survey of the manuscript sources then available and of the contributions of composers. An analysis of their notation practices serves as an aid in placing composers in their proper perspective.

————. "Intorno ad alcune musiche profane italiane del secolo XIV." *NM* I:2 (Dec. 1897), [?]–75.

Although this article is concerned chiefly with Paduan fragments, it is of general interest and importance, since it is one of the earliest known articles to deal with this subject.[23] It appears to be connected with the musical supplement of fifteen works of the Italian Ars Nova, here transcribed by Wolf for the first time. Page 75 of this same volume also contains what appears to be an editorial, "La nostra musica," regarding the supplement to follow. In a tribute to Professor Wolf, it is stated that Italian notation of the fourteenth century is little known, since nothing to date has been written about it and since there have heretofore been no transcriptions.[24]

————. "Italian Trecento music." *PMA* LVIII (1931), 15–31.

Today this paper, delivered at the Musical Association four decades ago, seems almost elementary and naive, as though the remarks were intended for a group of laymen. It might well demonstrate how far musicology has progressed since then and what noteworthy strides have been made in this particular area. Yet several points can still command attention: the general milieu, particularly Florence, the center of this activity; differing views regarding the etymology of the term "madrigal" and performance practice; the probability that Casella composed music and the speculation that Dante himself may possibly have also composed; the importance of the literary background, with reference to treatises dealing with metrical forms; the suggestion that perhaps the ballata was to be danced, and thus related to the estampida of the trovatori.

* ————, and H. Albrecht, eds. *Der Squarcialupi-Codex, Pal. 87 der biblioteca Medicea Laurenziana zu Florenz.* . . . Lippstadt, Kistner, & Siegel, 1955. Introduction.

A transcription of the entire Sq. Over 100 of the 352 pieces are published here for the first time, thus making a large body of Trecento music newly available. Introduction surveys briefly the musical culture of fourteenth-century Italy. Remarks on A. Squarcialupi and the composers represented. Annotations to the texts, and some explanation of the musical forms. Reviewed by (1) Fischer, *MF* IX (1956), 77–89; (2) Plamenac, *MQ* XLII (1956),

---

22. Main, 131.
23. Preceding it by one year is Gandolfi's "D'una ballata con musica . . . ," *NM* I:1 (1896), 1–3.
24. However, Gandolfi (*NM*, 1896) speaks of a transcription of Landini's "Angelica biltà" from Sq, appearing in the *Gazzetta Musicale di Milano* in 1848, by Casamorata (superius only). Fétis and Kiesewetter are known to have made early transcriptions of the same composer's "Non arà ma' pietà" (Fischer *32*, 61).

539–543; (3) Schrade, *Notes* XIII (1956), 683–688. The consensus is that the
publication is too "authentic" a reproduction, that there are errors in both
transcriptions and in Italian texts, and that the *Revisionsbericht* is much
too abbreviated. These shortcomings may be due in part to the fact that the
work was published posthumously.

FORMS (II)

An initial glance at the entries in the following section will reveal the inter-
disciplinary nature of musical forms and literary forms. As has already been
stated in the introduction, this bibliographic guide does not propose to go
deeply into literature; yet in studying the musical forms it is impossible to
divorce them from the literary ones. An effort has therefore been made to
limit the references in the latter area to writings that are truly indispensable
and that link the two disciplines. However, as an aid to the student who wishes
to make further investigations into the literary background, an appendix with
additional entries has been included (Appendix II).

Anglés, Higinio. "The Musical Notation and Rhythm of the Italian Laude."
In *Essays in Musicology: A Birthday Offering to Willi Apel*, ed. by Hans
Tischler. Bloomington, Indiana University School of Music, 1968, 51–60.
Lacking the international flavor of other European lyric monodies, the
Italian lauda in its simplicity more nearly resembles improvisation and
reflects the popular oral tradition. Those few laude that were passed down
with musical notation may look to the cantigas of Alphonso's thirteenth-
century Spain for a clue to their rhythmic interpretation. Transcriptions.

Apel, Willi. "Imitation in the Thirteenth and Fourteenth Centuries." In *Essays
in Honor of Archibald Davison*. Cambridge, Mass., Harvard University, De-
partment of Music, 1957, 25–38.
Unlike fourteenth-century France, where imitation practically disappears,
in Italy the basic texture of early fourteenth-century technique is the vocal duet, with parts proceeding in "ornamented conductus style." Rs is
cited as the earliest source, and those composers making most frequent use
of imitation are named.

Besseler *I* (1949). (I)

————— *II* (1931), 153–162. (I)

Bonaccorsi 2 (1948), 565–570. (I)

Bridgman, Nanie. "Lauda." *Musica* I:3 (1966), 93–94.

Brown, Howard. "Madrigale." *Musica* I:3 (1966), 227–229.

Cattin, Giulio. *Contributi alla storia della lauda spirituale; sulla evoluzione
musicale e letteraria della lauda nei secoli XIV e XV*. Bologna, 1958. (*Quadrivium, s.m.*, 2.)

The Ars Nova was the avant-garde of Italian musical culture, and the popularized lauda remained on the fringe of this movement. Lauda led to ballata: laude-ballate and ballate-travestite.

* Corsi, Giuseppe. "Madrigali e ballate inedite del Trecento." *Belfagor* XIV (1959), 72–82, 329–341.

This well-documented article points out that the madrigal developed in an essentially ecclesiastical atmosphere. Religious texts were often set to secular music, and thus we find secular pieces transformed into laude.

Damerini, Adelmo. "Lauda." *EM* II (1964), 574–575.

Debenedetti, Santorre. "Un trattatello del secolo XIV sopra la poesia musicale." *Studi medievali* II (1906–07), 59–82.

In which is translated the text of the anonymous *Capitulum* . . . , a treatise that sheds light on the poetic-musical forms in use in fourteenth-century Italy.

Ellinwood *1* (1960), 52–71. (I)

———— *4* (1939), xxv–xxx.

Fano, Fabio. "Ballata." *Musica* I:1 (1966), 316–318.

Fischer *4* (1961). (I)

———— *6* (1962). (I)

* Fischer. "Kontrafakturen und Parodien italienischen Werke des Trecento und frühen Quattrocento." *AM* V (1957), 43–59.

Regarding the interrelations between secular and sacred of the early Trecento, which reached their peak in the second half of the Quattrocento. Of the three forms, the ballata served the most often as a model for the sacred.

————. "Il madrigale." *EM* III (1964), 65.

———— *20* (1961). (I)

———— *32* (1956), 4–5. (I)

————. "Zur Ciconia-Forschung." *MF* XIV (1961), 316–322.

Some observations are made on the forms, with particular reference to Ciconia. Caccia would seem to stem from early period of *Trecentokunst* (ca. 1340), and Marrocco's dates of 1360–80 as peak are held questionable. Polyphonic ballata was in its beginnings during Ciconia's first Italian visit (1358–67).

Ghisi. "Gli aspetti musicali della lauda fra il XIV e il XV secolo, prima metà." In *Natalicia musicologica Knud Jeppesen,* ed. by Bjorn Hjelmborg and Søren Sørensen. Hafnia, W. Hansen, 1962, 51–57.

It is pointed out that a predominantly religious atmosphere, together with the secular music then winning favor, led to the transformation of the lauda. The religious text of the latter was set to the secular music of Landini and some of his contemporaries. Thus, to the same music we sometimes find two texts, one of religious character (lauda), the other of secular (madrigal or ballata). Fragments, transcribed.

———. "Caccia." *MGG* II (1952), 604–609.

The importance of the literary background is stressed, as well as that of the *Capitulum,* discovered by Debenedetti and expounded by Pirrotta *1.* As in the case of other terms (such as "fugue" later), the word "caccia" was generalized and applied to the contrapuntal art of canonic imitation. The caccia was entirely independent of the metrics of the text and was applied to the poetic form of the madrigal as well. There is a list of codices, containing "some twenty caccie," and of known composers.

——— *12* (1959). (I)

———. "Strambotti e laude nel travestimento spirituale della poesia musicale del Quattrocento." *CHM* I (1953), 45–78.

Regarding two laude derived from ballate, both partially transcribed.

* Ghislanzoni, Alberto. "Les formes littéraires et musicales italiennes au commencement du XIVᵉ siècle." *Wég* (1959), 149–163.

Concerning three early fourteenth-century treatises by Barberino, an anonymous writer (Venice, Bibl. Marciana Lat. cl. 12, n. 97), and da Tempo, which analyze the then current poetic forms and their varied musical adaptations. There are discussions of the origin of the early madrigal and the etymology of the term, and a comparison of the French chace with the Italian caccia. The three treatises are hailed as newly discovered aids in bridging the gap immediately preceding the Ars Nova period.

Handschin *1* (1948), 200–209. (I)

——— 2 (1931), 26–29. (I)

Includes etymology.

Karp, Theodore. "The Textual Origin of a Piece of Trecento Polyphony." *JAMS* XX (1967), 469–473.

This deals with the anonymous caccia, or canonic madrigal (Marrocco *3*), "Quant je voy . . . ," a unicum in FP. Speculation regarding its origin and chronology places it as a hybrid, the text being derived from a trouvère chanson. It is therefore neither truly Italianate nor entirely French.

Königslöw (1940), 3–10. (I)

* LiGotti. "L'Ars Nova e il madrigale." *Atti della reale accademia di scienze, lettere e arti di Palermo,* Ser. 4, Vol. IV:2 (1944), 339–389.

The madrigal is the typical form of the Italian Ars Nova. A list of all known madrigals of the fourteenth century and some composed in the early fifteenth serves as a primary contribution to the study of the madrigal. The list consists of text incipits with probable date of composition (cautiously suggested), metric schemes, poet and composer when known, codices, and where found in published form. A selection of complete texts progresses chronologically from Giovanni to Landini and Bartolino.

———— 5 (1944), 32–49.
With particular reference to the literary aspects.

* ————. "Poesie musicali italiane del sec. XIV." *Atti della reale accademia di scienze, lettere e arti di Palermo,* Ser. 4, Vol. IV:2 (1944), 99–167.
This deals with the importance of the texts. Text incipits of complete works of fourteen composers are listed. A cross section of the "poesie musicali" serves to demonstrate the change in taste and in style from the earlier period of Piero, Giovanni, and Jacopo to the later period of Andrea and Landini.

————. "Storia e poesia del *Pecorone.*" LiGotti *8* (1947), 140–157.

Liuzzi. "La ballata e la lauda." CorteA (1945), 62–68.
This sums up briefly what has been thoroughly developed in Liuzzi 2.

* ———— 2 (1935). (I)
In the Duecento the ballata imposes itself on the lauda. In the final decades of the Duecento and the early Trecento, ballata and lauda shared the element of a fresh popular spirit. Sincerity and simplicity of language reflect abundantly the contemporary customs.

————. "Melodie italiane inedite nel Duecento." *Archivum Romanicum* XIV:4 (1930), 327–560.
Regarding Jacopone da Todi in particular, and melodic schemes of laude, with music.

————. "Musica e poesia del Trecento nel codice Vaticano Rossiano 215." *Rendiconti della pontificia accademia romana di archaeologia* XIII:1–2 (1937), 59–71.
The lauda demonstrates the union of music and poetry in Italy before the Ars Nova.

————. "Profilo musicale di Jacopone." *La Nuova antologia* (1931), 171–192.
The lauda and Jacopone.

Luciani, Sebastiano A. "Le ballate ad una voce del Codice Squarcialupi." *Archivi d'Italia,* Ser. 2, Vol. III (1936), 60–66.
Underscores the importance of the eleven monodic ballate in Sq by Gherardello, Lorenzo, and Nicolò. Notwithstanding the art of the trouvères and trovatori, these represent the ultimate in monodic art. The rich melismatic melodies do not suggest instrumental performance (as Riemann holds), but are of Gregorian origin, which continued to influence both sacred and secular music until the sixteenth century.

Ludwig *3* (1930).
This author (as Besseler later) [25] feels that the French chace preceded and influenced the Italian caccia.

Main, Alexander. "Lorenzo Masini's Deer Hunt." In *The Commonwealth of Music . . . in Honor of Curt Sachs,* ed. by G. Reese and R. Brandel. New York: Free Press, 1965, 130–162.

———
25. Besseler *11*, 158.

General remarks on the interpretation of the caccia follow a presentation
of Lorenzo's "Apposte messe . . ." as a three-voiced canon throughout (including the ritornello). The structural plan is examined, and varying treat-
ments appearing in the five other notable transcriptions[26] are cited. It is
pointed out that at no time heretofore has this work been discussed.

Marrocco, W. Thomas. "The Ballata: A Metamorphic Form." *Acta* XXXI
(1959), 32–37.
> Traces the evolution of the ballata, from the thirteenth-century song-and-
> dance form through its development as a fourteenth-century art form, its
> alliance with the fifteenth-century frottola, and its emergence in the six-
> teenth century, when it becomes linked with the rejuvenated madrigal.
> This includes an analysis of the ballata form as an art song, with emphasis
> on the recurring refrain and on the ternary ABA form.

————. "The Enigma of the Canzone." *Speculum* XXXI (1956), 704–713.
> Regarding the character of the thirteenth- and fourteenth-century canzone.
> Author subscribes to the theory that the canzone of this period was not
> sung but was recited to an improvised instrumental accompaniment, and
> submits evidence to this effect. Well documented.

————, ed. *Fourteenth Century Italian Cacce.* 2d ed., rev. and expanded. Cambridge, Mass., Mediaeval Academy of America, 1961. (Mediaeval Academy of
America, 39.) Introduction.
> Carducci's thesis, as set forth in his *Cacce in rima,* is questioned, since the
> argument here is that a poem becomes a caccia only when it is set to music
> employing canonic devices. With Pirrotta it is agreed that the caccia, with
> its opening and closing melismas, concluding ritornello, and supporting
> third part, does not seem to have been influenced by the chace. It may well
> have preceded it.[27] Good exposition of the caccia and canonic madrigal,
> which should be studied with the transcriptions.

————. "The Fourteenth-Century Madrigal: Its Form and Content." *Speculum*
XXVI:3 (1951), 449–457.
> Concerning the etymology of the term "madrigal." Analysis of rhyme
> schemes and other devices of Trecento poets. Composers related to poets.

————, ed. *Italian Secular Music.* Monaco, Editions de l'Oiseau-Lyre, 1967, Vol.
VI, ix–x.

————. ed. *The Music of Jacopo da Bologna.* Berkeley and Los Angeles, University of California Press, 1954, 14–28.
> As an introduction to the works of Jacopo, the forms here discussed are
> related principally to his music. Logically, the emphasis is on the madrigal,
> since the main body of his work is in this genre.

Martinez *3* (1963). (I)

---

26. Husmann; Marrocco *3;* Pirrotta *26:*III; Wolf *5:*III; WolfSq.
27. Pirrotta *34:*I.

Monterosso, Raffaello. "La tradizione melismatica sino all'Ars Nova." *Cert* III (1970), 29–50.

> The monodic lauda of the Duecento.

Novati, Francesco. "Contributi alla storia della lirica musicale neolatina. Per l'origine e la storia della caccia." *Studi medievali* II (1906–07), 303–326.

Osthoff, Wolfgang. "Petrarca in der Musik des Abendlandes." *Castrum Peregrini* XX (Amsterdam, 1954), 5–19.

> The rhythmic structure of the madrigal binds the music to the text. Regarding etymology, *mandriale,* stemming from *mandra* (Herde) renders it originally a "shepherd's song." Melismas in the madrigal derive from southern Italy and Greece.

Parrish, Carl. "Giovanni da Firenze: Caccia, 'Con brachi assai.'" ParrishT, 76–78.

> An analysis of Giovanni's "Con brachi assai," together with the transcription that follows, displays the characteristics of the caccia.

Pirrotta, Nino. "Una arcaica descrizione trecentesca del madrigale." In *Festschrift Heinrich Besseler.* Leipzig, 1961, 155–161.

> A description and evaluation of the *Capitulum de vocibus applicatis verbis,*[28] whose anonymous author presumably looked on his work as a compendium, addressing it to nonmusicians. Yet it is no less useful than da Tempo's *Summa artis rithimicis . . .* toward an understanding of the Ars Nova, and indeed shows promise of shedding more light on the obscure origins of the early madrigal as well as on the early caccia (*caccie sive incalci*).

——. "Ballata." *EM* I (1963), 171–173.

——. "Ballata." *MGG* I (1949), 1157–1164.

> A clear exposition of the few early monodic ballate as found in Rs and Sq, contrasted with the numerous polyphonic ones produced during the height of Italian polyphony.

——. "Caccia." *EM* I (1963), 354–355.

——. "Due sonetti musicali del Trecento." In *Miscelánea en homenaje a monseñor Higinio Anglés.* Barcelona, 1958–1961, Vol. II, 651–662.

* ——. "Das Madrigal der Ars Nova: Etymologie, formale Gestaltung und Geschichte." *MGG* VIII (1960), 1419–1424.

> The still unresolved question of the etymology of "madrigal" is considered, and varying opinions in this area are presented. Importance of literary background is stressed, also that of Barberini's *Documenti d'amore.* "The polyphonic nature of the madrigal and the fact that its composers were almost without exception from ecclesiastical ranks speaks for its origins in ecclesiastical polyphony, from the conductus (Ludwig and

---

28. See also Ghislanzoni; also Debenedetti, "Un trattatello. . . ."

Ellinwood) or from Provençal organum (Besseler)." In the case of the early
madrigal, poet and composer were often the same, but by mid-century it
emerged as a literary form, attaining elegance and simplicity. Its musical
counterpart, though basically intended to be sung, often had instrumental
accessories, and in the case of the Faenza Codex was arranged for purely
instrumental performance.

———— 24 (1945). (I)

————. "Musica polifonica per un testo attribuito a Federico II." *Cert* II (1968),
97–108.
Regarding a two-voiced ballata, "Dolce lo mio drudo." This unicum, in
PR and thought to be anonymous, has the character of a siciliana, yet is
not without the features of the ballata. Poetry and music are analyzed,
and p. 109 contains the transcription.

————. "On Text Forms from Ciconia to Dufay." *ReeFest* (1966), 673–682.
Virelai and rondeau vis à vis Italian text forms.

* ————. "Per l'origine e la storia della caccia e del madrigale trecentesco."
RMI XLVIII (1946), 305–323; XLIX (1947), 121–142.
The theory is advanced that the madrigal may stem from monastic polyphony, since *matriale* comes from *matrialis*, which was perhaps the generic
term in use in ecclesiastical circles to denote compositions on secular texts.
Madrigal is contrasted with caccia. While the former has a florid upper
voice, supported by a tenor which is sung, the caccia's tenor (supporting
two canonic upper voices) is instrumental. Caccia has more archaic characteristics, is more artificial, and, contrary to appearances, is less lively.

————. "Piero e l'impressionismo musicale del secolo XIV." *Cert* I (1962), 57–
74.
This represents a changed view [29] regarding the role of the third voice
and the development of the caccia, which is now thought to have been
rapid. Piero more than any other composer contributed to this development. The appendix consists of a description of the five-voiced *cacie sive
incalci* described in the *Capitulum* vis à vis the Trecento caccia, which is
derived from the madrigal.

———— 36 (1935). (I)

————. "Sull'etimologia di 'madrigale.'" *Poesia* IX (1948), 60–61.
Unlike the lauda and ballata, the madrigal was exclusively polyphonic and
destined for a limited public possessing a degree of musical proficiency.
Since the ecclesiastics continued to be the custodians of the culture of the
Middle Ages, it must follow that the madrigal had its origins in an ec-
clesiastical atmosphere. *Cantus matricalis,* deriving from *matrix Ecclesia*
(Mother Church), could signify the sacred polyphony used by the singers
of the Church, in contrast with *cantus materialis,* with secular words.

Reaney *1* (1962), 292–300. (I)

---

29. Pirrotta *34.*

———— *12* (1970), 39, 54–55, 57. (I)

ReeM (1940), 362–368. (I)

Seay *2* (1965), 153–159. (I)

Toguchi, Kosaku. "Sulla struttura e l'esecuzione di alcune cacce arsnovistiche."
    Cert III (1970), 67–81.
> In which an attempt is made to credit the imitative technique of the
> archaic caccia (*cacie sive incalce,* as described in the *Capitulum*) with a
> contribution toward the Trecento caccia. "Ongni diletto" and "Or qua
> compagni" serve as musical examples, the former written out for six
> voices.

Vecchi *6* (1957). (I)

Wolf. "Die Rossi Handschrift 215 der Vaticana und das Trecento Madrigal." *PJ*
    XLV (1938), 53–69.
> A study of the contents of this oldest of the Trecento manuscripts includes
> descriptions of the early madrigal by Antonio da Tempo, Gidino da Som-
> macampagna, and the anonymous Venetian (*Capitulum* . . . , ed. by De-
> benedetti). Particularly enlightening is the excerpt from Da Tempo, trans-
> lated from the Latin, which suggests the hypothetical question, "In view of
> the fact that monodic madrigals are mentioned by Antonio da Tempo,
> could the monodic pieces in Rs perhaps be such monodic madrigals?"
> Transcriptions.

GEOGRAPHICAL DISTRIBUTION: GENERAL (III a)

Clercx *4*:I (1960), 20–27, 41–50. (I)

———— *7* (1956). (I)
> The focus here is on Padua, which is linked with other northern cities in
> this activity. Reasons for its importance are the possibility that Rs originated
> there and that Piero and Giovanni spent time there before going to Ve-
> rona. There is also, of course, Marchettus. Venice is linked with O.

Fischer *33* (1958), 188. (I)

Korte, Werner. "La musica nelle città dell'Italia settentrionale dal 1400 al
    1425." *RMI* XXXIX (1932), 513–530.
> Reconstruction of the repertory can be achieved by means of stylistic an-
> alysis, which equates composers to regions.

———— *2* (1933), 10–15, 75–89. (I)
> Particularly helpful in identifying some composers and in placing them
> chronologically and geographically.

Ludwig *1* (1904–5), 601. (I)

* Pirrotta *25* (1955). (I)

> Through a chain of events, names, and musical documents, it is demonstrated that the stream leads, without interruption, from the treatises and music of Marchettus at the Naples court to the appearance of the first generation of Italian Ars Nova composers in the northern courts. Then, in the second half of the Trecento, the center shifts to Florence.

* ———, ed. *Paola Tenorista in a New Fragment of the Italian Ars Nova.* Palm Springs, California, E. E. Gottlieb, 1961, 15–16.

> Regarding the early studies of Wolf, which showed a higher percentage of manuscripts in the Florentine tradition than those from the north. Yet even at that time Ludwig [30] questioned his colleague's view. Considering that a number of composers represented in the Florentine manuscripts were from the north and considering also the more recently discovered northern sources (Rs, Dom, and a new Padua manuscript, Pad D), we are now in a better position to read through the fallacy that Florence was the leader. Pirrotta states that the "Florentines were more often influenced than influencing."

———. "Scuole polifoniche italiane durante il secolo XIV: Di una pretesa scuola napolitana." *CHM* I (1953), 11–18.

> Only in Florence and perhaps Padua were there social conditions conducive to the development of local schools. But there was a tremendous efflorescence, and other cities are mentioned.

GEOGRAPHICAL DISTRIBUTION: SPECIFIC REGIONS (III b)

FLORENCE (Including Lucca, Perugia, Pisa, Pistoia, Siena)

Buck, August, and B. Becherini. "Florenz." *MGG* IV (1955), 367–394.

Carapetyan *1* (1957). (I; VII)

Cellesi, Luigia. "Documenti per la storia musicale di Firenze." *RMI* XXXIV (1927), 579–602; XXXV (1928), 553–582.

Davidsohn (1929). (I)

Luciani, Sebastiano A. *La musica in Siena.* Siena, Reale accademia senese degli Intronati, 1942.

Villani, Philippi. *Liber de origine civitatis Florentiae et eiusdem famosis civibus,* ed. by G. C. Galletti. Firenze, 1847, 1–100.[31]

Wesselofsky (*ca.* 1390, ed. 1867). (I)

---

30. Ludwig *1*, 601.
31. Or see Villani, *Le vite d'uomini illustri fiorentini* (Firenze, Sansone Coen, 1847), 46.

Wolf *3* (1945). (I)

———— *4* (1901–2). (I)

MILAN

Fano. "Origini della cappella musicale del Duomo di Milano. Il primo maestro di cappella: Matteo da Perugia (1402–16)." *RMI* LV (1953), 1–22.

Fano *3* (1956), 13–14. (I)
> To the effect that since secular polyphony found no favorable ground in Milan, there was no true Milanese composer.

Sartori, Claudio. "Matteo da Perugia e Bertrand Feragut." *Acta* XXVIII (1956), 12–27.

NAPLES (Including Aversa, Capua, Caserta)

Fischer *33* (1958), 188. (I)

Pirrotta *37* (1953). (III a)
> The periphery of Naples appears more important than Naples itself. The idea of a true Neapolitan school and of Naples as a center of activity is rejected.

PADUA

Clercx *7* (1956). (I; III a)

Fischer *33* (1958), 188. (I)

Pirrotta. *Il Codice Estense lat. 568 e la musica francese in Italia al principio del 1400.* Palermo, 1946. (Estratto degli *Atti della reale accademia di scienze, lettere e arti di Palermo*, Ser. 4, Vol. V:2.)

———— *25* (1955), 62, 64–68. (I; III a)

———— *26*:II (1960), i.

VENICE

Borren, Charles Van den. *Les débuts de la musique à Venise.* Bruxelles, Lombaerts, 1914, 12–20.

IDENTIFICATION AND ATTRIBUTION (IV)

Attribution is achieved by stylistic analysis; by a study of allusions in the texts to events, names, and places; and by a consideration of fourteenth-century heraldic devices and family emblems, which often yields clues to both attribution and chronology. Within recent years the last named of these techniques has gained in popularity,[32] and Bartolino and Paolo are among its most striking beneficiaries, for through its application new light has been shed on their lives and activities.[33]

Becherini *4* (1964).
    Concerning family crests and emblems, and the important role they played in Ars Nova poetic texts.

Borren, Charles Van den. "L'apport italien dans un manuscrit du XVe siècle, perdu et partiellement retrouvé." *RMI* XXXI (1924), 527–533. (V c)

Carducci *2* (1929), 309.

Clercx *7* (1956), 156–157. (I)

D'Accone, Frank. "Antonio Squarcialupi alla luce di documenti inediti." *Chigiana,* nuova ser. 3 (1966), 3–24.

Fischer *16* (1970), 23–26. (I)

————. *Paolo da Firenze und der Squarcialupi-Kodex.* Bologna, 1969. (*Quadrivium, s.m.,* 9.) (V b)

———— *25* (1970). (I)

———— *32* (1956), 7–9. (I)

Ghisi. "Italian Ars Nova Music: The Perugia and Pistoia Fragments of the Lucca Musical Codex and Other Unpublished Early 15th-Century Sources." *JRB* I:3 (1946), 173–191. (V b)

Gombosi (1950), 604. (I)

Günther, Ursula. "Die anonymen Kompositionen des Manuskripts Paris, B.N., fonds it. 568 (Pit)." *AfMW* XXIII (1966), 73–92. (V b)

Königslöw (1940), 11–36. (I)

Korte *2* (1933), 10–15, 75–89. (I)

LiGotti. "Per la biografia di due minori musicisti italiani dell' 'Ars Nova.' " LiGotti *8* (1947), 98–105.
    Emphasizes literary aspects. Deals with poets, but a section on composers also.

Marrocco *3* (1961), xviii. (II)

Nicholson, Edward W. B. "Introduction." In *Dufay and His Contemporaries,* ed. by John, J. F. R., and C. Stainer. London and New York, Novello, 1898), xiii–xix. (V c)
    Remarks on composers of the early fifteenth century and on the Papal choir of that period.

---

32. Among scholars employing this device are Becherini (*1, 4*) and Clercx (*4*:I). See also n. 33.
33. Goldine, Petrobelli, Thibault.

Pirrotta and LiGotti. "Il codice di Lucca." *MD* V (1951), 115–142.
Valuable information regarding some confusing names.

———— *26* (1954–1964). Forewords to all volumes.

Reaney. "The Italian Contribution to the Manuscript Oxford, Bodleian Library, Canonici Misc. 213." *Cert* III (1970), 443–464. (V c)

Thibault, Geneviève. "Emblèmes et devises des Visconti dans les oeuvres musicales du Trecento." *Cert* III (1970), 131–160.
A study of family crests and emblems can link music with society, and a strong case is made for wider use of this technique. By way of illustration are fourteen plates of family emblems (in this case those related to the Visconti), together with excerpts from texts that make reference to these, sometimes in an obscure manner.

Villani.

Wilkins, Nigel. "A Madrigal in Praise of the Della Scala Family." *RB* XIX (1965), 82–88.
Speculation regarding the attribution of the anonymous madrigal "La nobil Scala." Methods of stylistic analysis and allusion to family tend to rule out Bartolino and Giovanni and to favor Jacopo. Transcription.

Wolf. "Dufay und seine Zeit." *SIMG* I (1899–1900), 150–163.
Concerning composers of different nationalities, including Italian. Location of manuscripts is related to establishment of names.

———— *4* (1902), 609–613. (I)

———— *5*:I (1904), 228–273. (I)

———— Sq (1955), Introduction (viii–xiii). (I)

MANUSCRIPT SOURCES: GENERAL (V a)

Since the manuscripts were always compiled some years after their contents had been composed, there is some disagreement among scholars regarding chronology. Exemplifying this wide disagreement are the views of Fischer and Pirrotta, the latter invariably dating them two or three decades after the former. Most conspicuous in this area are the cases of Rs, the earliest, and Sq, the latest of the principal sources.

Besseler *1* (1949), 705–706. (I)

———— *13:I* (1925), 226–234. (I)

* Borren *9* (1941), 49–59. (I)

Clercx *4*:I (1960), 64–81. (I)

————. "Johannes Ciconia et la chronologie des manuscrits italiens, Mod. 568 et Lucca (Mn)." *Wég* (1959), 110–130.

—— 7 (1956), 156–157. (I)

Ellinwood *1* (1960), 45–48. (I)

—— *4* (1939), xvii–xx.

Ficker *2* (1960), 142–143 ,149–152.

Fischer. "Chronologie des manuscrits du Trecento." *Wég* (1959), 131–136.
A discussion of chronology, based on Fischer *32*.

—— *6* (1962), 18–31. (I)

——. "L'influence française sur la notation des manuscrits du Trecento."
Wég (1959), 27–34.

——. "Neue Quellen zur Musik des 13., 14., und 15. Jahrhunderts." *Acta*
XXXVI (1964), 83–84. (V c)

* —— *32* (1956), 10–11, 88–103. (I)

—— *33* (1958), 181–185. (I)

——. "Ein Versuch zur Chronologie von Landinis Werken." *MD* XX (1966),
31–46. (VIII a)

LiGotti *5* (1944), 56–65. (I)

Ludwig *1* (1904–05), 613–619. (I)

——, ed. *Guillaume de Machaut. Musikalische Werke*. Vol. II. Introduction.
Leipzig, Breitkopf & Härtel, 1928, 24.

—— *4* (1902–03), 52–59. (I)

Marrocco *6*:VI (1967), ix.

—— 7 (1954), 5–13. (II)

Pirrotta *12* (1959), 95–97. (I)
Chronology.

* —— *33* (1961), 15–20. (III a)

—— *36* (1935), 38, nn. 1 and 2. (I)

Wolf *5*:I (1904), 228–273. (I)

—— 7 (1897). (I)

—— Sq (1955), Introduction (i–viii). (I)

MANUSCRIPT SOURCES: MAJOR (V b)

It will be noted in the following pages that manuscript abbreviations follow
the manuscript title in parentheses. The first abbreviation is that selected for
use in this work; the following ones are varying symbols in use by other writers to designate the same manuscript. In the case of each manuscript, I have

indicated, as nearly as possible, the number of works (Italian secular) by named composers,[34] and the number of anonymous works, as well as the number of those transcribed. But it must be pointed out that since 1964 (first edition of this guide) many more of these compositions have been transcribed, and a number of those of questionable attribution have now been identified. Since this process continues at a rapid rate, the following statistics cannot be taken as final. Any remaining compositions of questionable attribution are so indicated within brackets.

FAENZA, BIBL. COMUNALE 117 (Faenza; Fa; Bonadies)

* Borren, Charles Van den. "Le codex de Johannes Bonadies, musicien du XVe siècle." *Revue belge d'archéologie et d'histoire de l'art* X (1940), 251–261. (VI)

> These are the first observations to be made on this codex of anonymous keyboard music, first known in 1870 as Codex Bonadies, then forgotten until 1937.

Carapetyan, Armen, ed. *An Early Fifteenth-Century Italian Source of Keyboard Music: The Codex Faenza, Biblioteca Comunale, 117.* A facsimile edition. N.p. American Institute of Musicology, 1961. (Musicological Studies and Documents, 10.) Foreword.

> To the effect that this codex (known earlier as *Bonadies*) represents a landmark in the history of early keyboard music. It is agreed with Plamenac that this unique collection of instrumental elaborations of French and Italian Trecento music was very likely written sometime before 1420. A facsimile edition of Faenza is also found in *MD* XIII (1959), 79–107; XIV (1960), 67–104; and XV (1961), 65–104.

\# Kugler, M. "Die Tastenmusik im Codex Faenza." Doctoral dissertation, Munich, 1970. (Unpublished?)

Marrocco *6*:VI (1967), 172.

> It is observed that five of the keyboard compositions in this codex are paraphrases on tenors taken from Jacopo by an anonymous late fourteenth-century arranger.

Plamenac, Dragan. "Alcune osservazioni sulla struttura del codice 117 della biblioteca communale di Faenza." *Cert* III (1970), 161–175.

> Of special interest is the mention of paraphrases on madrigali and ballate of Jacopo, Bartolino, Landini, and Zacara da Teramo, contained in the second section of the codex. Plates of ten facsimiles and instrumental versions of two other Italian ballate are contained in Section 1.

———. "Faenza, Codex 117." *MGG* III (1954), 1709–1714.

———. "Faventina." In *Liber Amicorum Charles Van den Borren,* ed. by Albert Van der Linden. Anvers, Lloyd Anversois, 1964, 145–164.

---

34. By "named composers" is meant that in the particular manuscript in question the composition bears a name, or is attributed to a certain composer.

Following some remarks on the history of this codex of anonymous keyboard works based on religious and secular vocal compositions, this deals
principally with an instrumental paraphrase on the anonymous ballata,
"Deduto sey," from Pz and Bu, never before published. Speculation regarding the composition is followed by a facsimile of the same, together
with the transcription.

* ———. "Keyboard Music of the Fourteenth Century in Codex Faenza 117."
JAMS IV (1951), 179–201.[35] (VI)

* ———. "New Light on the Codex Faenza 117." *RIMS* (Utrecht, 1952), 310–
326.
"It is unlikely that this codex was compiled after 1420." As a collection of
late Gothic instrumental music, it demonstrates the preeminent positions
of both France and Italy in the area of instrumental as well as vocal
music. Here the earlier view is sustained, i.e., that score notation would
indicate that these are for a keyboard instrument and were very likely
intended for the personal use of a keyboard player. Instrumental transcription of Zacara da Teramo's "Un fior gentil" and "Rosetta. . . ."

———. "A Note on the Rearrangement of the Faenza Codex 117." *JAMS*
XVII:1 (spring 1964), 78–81.
An explanation and clarification of the rearrangement of the codex as it
appears in the facsimile edition as found in Carapetyan 2 and an announcement of a forthcoming edition in transcription. Some interesting information regarding the background of this manuscript.

Roncaglia, Gino. "Intorno ad un codice di Johannes Bonadies." *Atti e memorie
della reale accademia di scienze, lettere ed arti di Modena,* Ser. 5, Vol.
IV (1939), 39 ff.

FLORENCE, BIBL. MEDICEA LAURENZIANA, Pal. 87 (Sq; Pal. 87; Squarcialupi; FL; S) [36]
351 works by named composers, all transcribed in a complete edition
(WolfSq). Questions related to the chronology of this richest and latest
of the principal Trecento sources continue to incite dispute. This centers
largely around the style of handwriting and the person who directed its
compilation. Principal participants in this duel are Fischer and Pirrotta.
See in particular Fischer 22 and 32 and Pirrotta *10:III* and *12*.

* Becherini, Bianca. "Antonio Squarcialupi e il codice Mediceo Palatino 87."
Cert I (1962), 140–180.
Seeks further clarification of Squarcialupi's relationship to the codex. Sub-

35. Announced in 1968, "In preparation": *Keyboard Music of the Middle Ages Era
in Faenza Bibl. Comunale, Codex 117* (American Institute of Musicology, *CMM*).
36. References here also include works about A. Squarcialupi, who, although he
lived in the Quattrocento and "has nothing in common with the music of the Ars
Nova" (Becherini *1,* 166), was the possessor and no doubt the promoter of the codex
(Pirrotta *25,* 71).

mits documentation supporting the theory that he was not the compiler. Perhaps Paolo was?

———— 2 (1962), 49–51.

————. "Communications sur Antonio Squarcialupi et notes au Cod. Palatino 87." *RIMS* (Köln, 1958), 65.
This seeks to refute the popular notion that this codex belonged to the well-known Squarcialupi family and proposes that someone married into the family perhaps presented it to "Antonio degli Organi," who was himself of humble origins.

D'Accone *1* (1966).

D'Ancona, Paolo. *La miniatura fiorentina (sec. XI–XVI).* Firenze, Olschki, 1914, 175.

Ellinwood *1* (1960), 47. (I)

———— *4* (1939), xvii–xviii. (VIII a)

Fischer *5* (1959), 134–135. (V a)

———— *16* (1970), 27. (I)

———— *22* (1969).
Additional clues are enumerated regarding the circumstances of compilation: (1) resemblance between Fl 999 (which contains a *Gaudeamus* of Paolo) and Sq; (2) the writing, or at least the illumination, of Sq in Santa Maria degli Angeli; (3) 1419 as the death date of Paolo; (4) the connection of Paolo not only with the Capponi but with Uzzano, Bartholi, and Leoni. These findings support Fischer's earlier thesis that Sq was compiled in 1415–1419, and that Paolo and his immediate circle were deeply involved in its compilation.

————. "Squarcialupi, Antonio." *MGG* XII (1965), 1096–1097.

————. "Squarcialupi Codex." *MGG* XII (1965), 1097–1100.

————. "Der Squarcialupi-Codex. . . ." *MF* IX (1956), 77–89.
A review of the Wolf edition, with a list of corrections.

———— *32* (1956), 93–95. (I)

Gandolfi *2* (1892). (I)

Ghisi. "Poesie musicali italiane. . . ." *NA* XV (1938), 36–41, 189–196, 271–280.
A comparative analysis of identical compositions found in both Sq and FP (see below) to establish points of difference in manner of writing.

LiGotti *5* (1944), 63–65. (I)

Luciani *1* (1936). (II)

Ludwig *1* (1904–05), 613–614. (I)

———— *4* (1902–03), 56–57. (I)

Pirrotta *10:III* (1951), 119 n. 13. (IV)
In referring to the rich illuminations and to the style of handwriting,

Pirrotta calls this "A collection of humanistic character, not designed for practical use," and maintains it cannot predate 1440.

———— *12* (1959), 95 n. 2.

Four years later (actually in 1955) the author defends his stand of "not before 1440" on the grounds that such rich illuminations as those contained in Sq were found prior to 1440 only in religious manuscripts, that the Gothic hand may have been a deliberate attempt to conform to the Trecento character of the contents, that Squarcialupi's name itself appears in the manuscript in Gothic characters, and that he himself no doubt directed its compilation.

———— *25* (1955), 71. (I)

Taucci, Raffaello. *Fra Andrea dei Servi, organista e compositore del Trecento.* Roma, Collegio S. Alessio Falconieri, 1935. (Estratto dalla *Rivista di studi storici sull'Ordine de Servi di Maria,* A.II, 1935), 23–24. (VIII a)

Wolf *5:*I (1904), 228–244. (I)
Brief history and inventory.

* ———— Sq (1955), Introduction.

A brief survey of the musical culture of fourteenth-century Italy, with remarks on Antonio Squarcialupi and on the composers represented in the codex. Speculation regarding the date of compilation would place it not earlier than the first decade of the fifteenth century, but the possible identification of N. Zacherie with Zacherias Cantor of 1420 could result in establishing a more specific date. It is pointed out that the collection runs the gamut of the various phases of the development of mensural notation. Included also are annotations to the texts together with some explanation of the musical forms.

FLORENCE, BIBL. NAZIONALE CENTRALE, Panc. 26 (FP; Panc. 26; FP 26)

151 by named composers, transcribed [37]

Becherini *2* (1962), 51. (I)

Ellinwood *4* (1939), xviii. (VIII a)

Fischer *5* (1959), 131–132. (IV a)

———— *32* (1956), 88–90. (I)

Ghisi *13* (1938), 36–41, 189–196, 271–280.[38]

LiGotti *5* (1944), 58–59. (I)

Ludwig *1* (1904–05), 614. (I)

———— *2* (1928), 28.

Pirrotta. "Codex Palatino Panciatichiano 26 (FP)." *MGG* IV (1955), 401–405.

---

37. There is at least one work of questionable attribution. The caccia "Segugi a corta" is treated by Fischer (*32*, 38) as anonymous. Marrocco in *3*, 23 a/b attributed it to Piero but now is doubtful, as is Pirrotta (*26:*II, 43).

38. See under Sq for annotation.

———— *33* (1961), 16–17. (III a)

Schrade, Leo, ed. *The Works of Francesco Landini.* Monaco, Editions de l'Oiseau-Lyre, 1958. Commentary, 6–7. (VIII a)

Taucci (1935), 23. (VIII a)

Wolf *5*:I (1904), 244–250. (I)
Brief description and inventory. Some comparison with contents of other codices.

LONDON, BRITISH MUSEUM, add. 29987 (Lo; L)

81 [?] by named composers,[39] 77 transcribed
10 [?] anonymous works, 9 transcribed

Ellinwood *1* (1960), 46. (I)

———— *4* (1939), xix. (VIII a)

Fischer *32* (1956), 90–92. (I)

LiGotti *5* (1944), 61–62. (I)

Marrocco *7* (1954), 6, 13. (VIII a)

Pirrotta *26*:II (1960), ii.

* Reaney. "The Manuscript London, B.M., Additional 29987 (Lo)." *MD* XII (1958), 67–91.
Description and origins, contents, composers, concordances, inventory, bibliography.

————, ed. *The Manuscript London, B.M., Additional 29987, A Facsimile Edition.* American Institute of Musicology, 1965. (*Musicological Studies and Documents, 13.*)

————. "Die wichtige Trecento-Hs. *Add 29987 (Lo).* . . ." *MGG* VIII (1960), 1185–1187.

Wolf *5*:I (1904), 268–273. (I)

LUCCA,[40] ARCHIVIO DI STATO, ms. 184 (Luc; MANCINI; Man; Mn) [41]

40 [+3]? by named composers, all transcribed (incl. Perugia and Pistoia fragments)
18 [+1]? anonymous, 16 transcribed [42]

---

39. As Reaney (7, 72) points out, because of the frequent omissions of composers' names it is often difficult to draw definite conclusions regarding attribution.

40. The first edition of this guide listed this codex with Other Sources, but further thought and study has led me to place it now among the major sources.

41. Clercx refers to this codex as "le manuscrit Mancini" (Clercx *6*, 115), which would then embrace the Lucca, Perugia, and Pistoia fragments. She prefers the approach of Ghisi (*10*, 174, 178) and Pirrotta (*10:I*, 119), namely, "Lucca Codex (Mancini)," with its Perugia and Pistoia fragments.

42. The anonymous ballata, "Mercé o morte," from the Pistoia fragment, which is also in BU (see Fischer *32*, 58) and transcribed by Ghisi (*11*, 17), is not included in the Pirrotta inventory. Disertori ascribes "De mia farina . . ." to Antonellus.

This source is also called the Mancini Codex, after the discoverer of the Lucca portion (in 1935), which constitutes the main body of the manuscript. The problems posed by this codex have been singularly acute, not only because of the physical separation of its three portions but more importantly because much of it is in a condition of severe mutilation. As early as 1938 Professor Ghisi wrote of the Pistoia fragment, and in 1946 he undertook to fit the Perugia fragment into its proper position in the Lucca portion. In 1949 (*MD* III) Nino Pirrotta went still further in collating it and, together with LiGotti (*MD* III, IV, and V), published an inventory, as well as the literary texts.

Bonaccorsi *2* (1948), 572–608, 614–615. (I)

Bukofzer, Manfred. "Two Mensuration Canons." *MD* II (1948), 165–171.
Expresses some disagreement with Ghisi (Ghisi *10*).

Clercx *4*:I (1960), 65–67. (I)

——— *6* (1959), 115–122.

Fischer. "Lucca, Codex." *MGG* VIII (1960), 1249–1251.

——— *32* (1956), 96–97. (I)

——— *33* (1958), 181–182. (I)

Ghisi. "Bruchstücke einer neuen Musikhandschrift der italienischen Ars Nova."
AfMW VII (1942), 17–39.
The Perugia fragment (PerBC). Considerations of style and notation, with an analysis of some of the works. Remarks on composers and poets. Three musical transcriptions.

———. "Frammenti di un nuovo codice musicale dell'Ars Nova italiana." *La Rinascità* V (1942), 72–103.
Same as Ghisi *5*, but here without music. The two cacce (transcribed in Ghisi *5*) from the mid-fifteenth century are submitted as evidence of the evolution of the caccia; they are from PerBC and BL Q16, both anonymous.

———. "Un frammento musicale dell'Ars Nova italiana nell'Archivio capitolare della cattedrale di Pistoia." *RMI* XLII:2 (1938), 162–168.
Regarding the Pistoia fragment.

* ——— *10* (1946).
Subtitled "The Perugia and Pistoia fragments of the Lucca musical codex and other unpublished early fifteenth-century sources." Reconstruction of these fragments establishes the connection between them and indicates that they form a part of the Lucca collection.

Mancini, Augusto. "Frammenti di un nuovo codice dell'Ars Nova." *Rendiconti dell'accademia nazionale dei Lincei*, Ser. 8, Vol. II (1947), 85–94.
Concerning the Lucca portion. Valuable bibliographical footnotes.

* Pirrotta and E. LiGotti. "Il codice di Lucca." *MD* III (1949), 119–138.
Description and inventory, including concordances.

* ——— and ———. "Il codice di Lucca." *MD* IV (1950), 111–152.
Literary texts.

* —— and ——. "Il codice di Lucca." *MD* V (1951), 115–142.
Repertoire, composers. A comprehensive and penetrating study.

PARIS, BIBL. NATIONALE, fonds italien 568 (Pit; P)

138 by named composers, all transcribed
26 [?] anonymous works, all transcribed

Clercx *4*:I (1960), 79. (I)

Ellinwood *1* (1960), 46. (I)

—— *4* (1939), xx. (VIII a)

Fétis, François. *Biographie universelle des musiciens.* . . . 1st ed. Paris, Firmin-Didot, 1835, Introduction, 195–199.

* ——. "Découverte des manuscrits intéressans." *Revue musicale* I (1827), 107–113.
This article is of special interest, since it appeared the year of the discovery of the manuscript (1827) and speculates that it was written "between 1350 and 1430"!

Fischer *32* (1956), 92–93. (I)

* Günther *1* (1966).
Until recently some twenty-six Italian compositions had remained without attribution because of puzzling abbreviations and apparent erasures. But by means of treatment with infrared rays, a comparison of hands and signatures has become possible. As a result, it is held that some sixteen works are now attributable, very likely twelve of them to Paolo. Bärenreiter announces a facsimile edition "soon."

——. "Zur Datierung des Madrigals 'Godi Firenze' und der Handschrift Paris, B. N. fonds it. 568 (Pit)." *AfMW* XXIV:2 (May 1967), 99–119.
To the effect that the compilers of Pit put an emphasis on Paolo's work; therefore it is reasonable to agree with Pirrotta [43] that there was a connection with the Capponi family, who in turn had connections with the Camaldolese. The oldest fascicle of Pit is thought to date from 1405–06; the most recent one from 1408.

LiGotti *5* (1944), 62–63. (I)

Ludwig *1* (1904–05), 615. (I)

—— *2* (1928), 27.

Pirrotta *33* (1961), 17–18; 19 n. 21. (V a)

* Reaney. "The Manuscript Paris, Bibliothèque Nationale, fonds italien 568 (Pit)." *MD* XIV (1960), 33–63.
Regarding the importance of this manuscript, and Paolo's close connection with it. Description and origins, contents, composers, tables, bibliography, inventory (including concordances). Compiled "shortly after 1400."

---

43. Pirrotta *33*, 25–26. See also Fischer *22* for Paolo and the Capponi family.

Reaney. "Pariser Handschriften," *MGG* X (1962), 796–797.

Thibault [?].[44]

Wolf *5:*I (1904), 250–258. (I)

PARIS, BIBL. NATIONALE, Nouv. acq. franç. 6771 (PR; Reina; R) Italian
part: fasc. 1–5

> 72 [+3] works by named composers, transcribed
> 29 [−3] anonymous works, 28 transcribed [45]

Ellinwood *1* (1960), 46–47. (I)

——— *4* (1939), xix–xx. (VIII a)

Fischer. "Drei unbekannte Werke von Jacopo da Bologna und Bartolino da
Padova?" *Miscelánea en homenaje a monseñor Higinio Anglés,* I (Barcelona,
1958–1961), 265–281.

* ———. "The manuscript Paris, Bibl. nat., nouv. acq. frç. 6771." *MD* XI (1957),
38–78.
> Description and origins, composers, forms, concordances, notation and
> language, bibliography, inventory.

———. "Reina, Codex." *MGG* XI (1963), 179–181.

———. "A Reply to N. E. Wilkins' Article on the Codex Reina." *MD* XVII
(1963), 75–77.
> States that the absence of Ciconia's work here is an argument against Padua
> as seat of origin. Agrees with Wilkins that PR is a monument to the close
> contact between French and Italian musical culture in the late fourteenth
> and early fifteenth centuries. Lists important corrections of his earlier in-
> ventory.

——— *32* (1956), 95–96. (I)

——— *33* (1958), 180, 184, 194. (I)

Günther, Ursula. "Der Gebrauch des tempus perfectum diminutum in der Handschrift Chantilly 1047." *AfMW* XVII (1960), 288–289.
> Regarding the Italianisms contained in a French text found in both PR
> and Chantilly (Musée Condé, 564 [olim 1047]), indicating that the same
> scribe wrote both, as well as some of the Italian portion of PR, and that he
> was familiar with both the French and the Italian languages and notation
> systems.

LiGotti *5* (1944), 59–60. (I)

Ludwig *1* (1904–05), 616. (I)

---

44. Günther *1* refers to a paper on this manuscript read at Wégimont in 1962 by
Mme de Chambure. This has apparently not been published.

45. Fischer *7,* by means of a stylistic analysis of three *unica* in this codex, submits
evidence that two are by Jacopo and one by Bartolino. Since these had hitherto been
considered anonymous, this would now alter the proportion, and I have indicated
these differences within brackets.

—— *2* (1928), 24–25.

—— *4* (1902–03), 53–54. (I)

Marrocco *6:*VI (1967), ix. (II)

Pirrotta *26:*II (1960), ii.

Reaney *13* (1962), 796–797.

* Wilkins, Nigel. "The Codex Reina: A Revised Description." *MD* XVII (1963), 57–73.

    A reexamination in disagreement with Fischer's view as expressed in 1957 (Fischer *15*). In view of the circumstances of compilation, Padua and not Venice is suggested as the place where it was copied. Interplay of French and Italian is emphasized. Some facsimiles of both French and Italian works.

* ——, ed. *A Fourteenth-Century Repertory from the Codex Reina.* American Institute of Musicology, 1966. (CMM, 36.) Introduction.

    The history and description of the physical condition of the manuscript are followed by a brief evaluation of all previous studies made on this source, which so clearly reflects the close relationship between northern Italy and southeastern France at the close of the fourteenth century. Again it is strongly felt that fascicles I and II were assembled at Padua because of the watermarks on the paper. Transcriptions are all of French works.

Wolf *5:*I (1904), 260–267 (provisional). (I)

ROME, BIBL. VATICANA, Rs (Rossi; Rossi 215). Now includes the Ostiglia fragment, RsO

    4 by named composers, transcribed

    32 [or 29?] anonymous works, 29 transcribed

The majority of scholars appear to agree that the contents of this earliest of sources probably stem from *ca.* 1330–1340, though Strunk gives the dates as 1320–1330. The continued disagreement between Fischer and Pirrotta seems to center more on the date of compilation, the former placing it shortly before 1350 and the latter about 1370.

Apel, Willi. *The Notation of Polyphonic Music, 900–1600.* 5th ed. Cambridge, Mass., Mediaeval Academy of America, 1953, 382. (VII)

Besseler *1* (1949), 719–720. (I)

—— *13:II* (1926), 233–234.

    Inventory (including concordances).

Borghezio, G. "Un codice vaticano trecentesco di rime musicali." *Fédération archéologique et historique de Belgique* (Bruges), 1925, 231–232.

Ellinwood *1* (1960), 45. (I)

Fischer *32* (1956), 95. (I)

LiGotti *5* (1944), 25–31. (I)

Liuzzi *4* (1937), 50–71. (II)

Marrocco. "The Newly Discovered Ostiglia Pages of the Vatican Rossi Codex: The Earliest Italian *Ostinato.*" *Acta* XXXIX (1967), 84–91.
  A listing of the contents of the Ostiglia fragment ("Raccolta Greggiati'), amounting to eight additional unica, all anonymous. A description of the recently discovered pages is followed by a transcription of the madrigal "E con chaval," which appears to be the earliest example of variation form over ostinato.

Martinez *3* (1963). (I)

Mischiati, Oscar. "Uno sconosciuto frammento appartenente al codice Vaticano Rossi 215." *RIM* I:1 (1966), 68–76.
  Regarding the author's discovery in the Greggiati Collection at Ostiglia of two leaves of Rs, the "oldest musical manuscript." A complete transcription of the manuscript is in progress. Bibliography is useful.

Pirrotta *12* (1959), 95 (incl. n. 1). (I)

——— *22* (1936). (I)

——— *25* (1955), 64, 67–68. (I)
  With specific reference to the notation, which is more archaic than that of the "first generation" of Ars Nova composers.

* ——— *26*:II (1960), i–ii.

——— *33* (1961), 59. (V a; VIII a)

Sesini, Ugo. "Il canzoniero musicale trecentesco del cod. Vat. Rossiano 215." *Studi medievali* (N.S.) XVI (1943–50), 212–236.

Steiner, M. "Ein Beitrag zur Notationsgeschichte des frühen Trecento: Die Lehren des Marchettus von Padua und der Codex Rossiano 215." Unpublished [?] doctoral dissertation, Vienna, 1931.

Strunk *1* (1950). (I)

Toguchi, Kosaku. "Studio sul Codice Rossiano 215 della biblioteca vaticana; intorno al sistema della sua notazione musicale." *Annuario dell instituto giapponese di cultura* I (Rome, 1963), 169–184.

* Vecchi, Giuseppe, ed. *Il canzoniere musicale del Codice Vaticano Rossi 215 con uno studio sulla melica italiana del Trecento.* Vol. I. Bologna, Università degli studi di Bologna, 1965. (*Monumenta lyrica medii aevi italica*, 3) Facsimile edition. Introduction.
  This highly significant collection of Italian lyrical works is the earliest *musical* manifestation of the cultural climate created by Dante and Petrarch and was no doubt produced in the vicinity of Padua and Verona. The recent discovery of the Ostiglia fragments (included in this facsimile edition) has been a substantial aid in the continuing reconstruction of this precious codex.

* Wolf *12* (1938). (II)

The significance of this earliest known source is stressed. There follow a physical description, study of the literary background, comparison with other codices, brief inventory with provisional "concordances," musical examples, and four compositions, transcribed.

MANUSCRIPT SOURCES: OTHERS (V c) [46]

It will be observed that some of the manuscripts in the following section are of considerable proportions, while others, for our purposes, are of minor consequence. Italian secular vocal compositions found their way into many manuscripts or manuscript fragments on the continent, and a number of these belong to a later period. In addition to the larger ones, we have included those that have held particular attraction for scholars and those that contain one or more *unica,* as in the case of Cas. Other minor codices are not considered here.[47]

BERLIN FRAGMENT, DEUTSCHE STAATSBIBL. DER STIFTUNG PREUSSISCHER KULTURBESITZ, cod. lat. 4°523 (Ber)

1 ballata, transcribed

Fischer. "Una ballata trecentesca sconosciuta." *Cert* II (1968), 39–42.

Concerning the ballata by Fr[anciscus] Reynaldus (see below). Transcription.

———— *17* (1964), 83 ff.

Regarding a hitherto unknown ballata by Fr[ancisus] Reynaldus. Notation precedes 1400, and style resembles that of Landini or of Andreas. Facsimile.

BOLOGNA, CIVICO MUSEO BIBLIOGRAFICO MUSICALE, Q15 (olim Liceo musicale 37) (BL)

"2 Italian secular"[?] [48]

Besseler. "Bologna Kodex BL." *MGG* II (1952), 95–99.

---

46. It must be remembered that this is essentially a guide to modern editions, and that therefore the study of the manuscripts is not pursued to its furthermost limits. Occasionally there may be a variation of one or two in the number of compositions in a codex, depending on the findings of different scholars. Besseler *13*, Fischer *32*, and the inventories in *MD* have served as principal guides.

47. For a list of these, see Manuscripts and Their Sigla, p. 9; see also Fischer *32*, 10, 97, 102–103.

48. Clercx (*4:*I, 68) refers to some secular works that found their way into this manuscript, and Besseler (*13:*I, 234) has stated that it contains two Italian secular compositions in a supplement. Could these be the laude derived from ballate, of which Ghisi writes (Ghisi *16*, 49)?

—————— *13:I* (1925), 234–236. (I)

Clercx *4:*I (1960), 67–71. (I)

Ficker *2* (1960), 150.

Ghisi *16* (1953), 49. (II)
    Regarding two laude derived from ballate, both partially transcribed.

Ludwig *2* (1928), 20.

Van, Guillaume de. "Inventory of the Manuscript Bologna Liceo Musicale, Q 15
    (olim 37)." *MD* II (1948), 231–257.
    Strictly an inventory (with concordances).

Wolf *5:*I (1904), 197–198.

BOLOGNA, BIBL. UNIVERSITARIA 2216 (BU)

    8 anonymous works, all transcribed

Besseler. "Bologna Kodex BU," *MGG* II (1952), 99–101.

—————. "The Manuscript Bologna Biblioteca Universitaria 2216." *MD* VI
    (1952), 39–65.
    Description and origins, comparison with other manuscripts, contents, com-
    posers, tables, bibliography, inventory (including concordances). Observa-
    tions on the two Bologna manuscripts and on their importance.

Gallo, F. Alberto. *Il codice musicale 2216 della Biblioteca Universitaria di
    Bologna.* Bologna, 1968–70. 2 vols.
    Vol. I: Facsimile edition. Vol. II: Historical introduction, a new inventory,
    and transcriptions.

—————. "Musiche veneziane nel ms. 2216 della Biblioteca Universitaria di
    Bologna." *Quadrivium* VI (1964), 107–111.

Ludwig *1* (1904–05), 618–619. (I)

Wolf *5:*I (1904), 198–208. (I)

DOMODOSSOLA FRAGMENTS, CONVENTO DI MONTE CALVARIO, MS
14, now at Stresa, Collegio Rosmini (Dom) [49]

    4 by named composers, 3 transcribed
    1 anonymous work, transcribed

Besseler *13:II* (1926), 230.

Clercx *7* (1956), 156–157. (I)

Ghisi *10* (1946), 183.

Ludwig *1* (1904–05), 640. (I)

———

49. Paduan fragment? (Plamenac *2,* 166.)

Plamenac. "Another Paduan Fragment of Trecento Music." *JAMS* VIII (1955), 165–181.

Sabbadini, Remiglio. "Frammenti di poesie volgari musicate." *Giornale storico della letteratura italiana* XL (1902), 270.

   Pertaining to three musical settings, by Jacobus Corbus, Johannes Ciconia, and Zaninus de Peraga de Padua.

ESCORIAL IV. α. 24 (Esc; EscB)

   1 anonymous work, transcribed

GROTTAFERRATA, BIBL. DELLA BADIA GRECA E. β. XVI. Fragment (Grot) [50]

   4 by named composers, transcribed

Corsi, Giuseppe. "Frammenti di un codice musicale dell'Ars Nova rimasti sconosciuti." *Belfagor* XX:2 (1965), 210–215.

Fischer. "Ein neues Trecentofragment." In *Festschrift für Walter Wiora*, ed. by L. Finscher and C. H. Mahling. Basel and New York, Bärenreiter, 1967, 264–268.

   Relevant to this guide is the presence of three madrigals and one ballata (by Jacopo, Giovanni, and Landini, respectively) in this newly discovered fragment (1965).

IVREA, BIBL. CAPITOLARE, COD. 104

Fischer *17* (1964), 84.

   Among the early fifteenth-century works in this fragment is a ballata in three-part notation, with words in the tenor, "De vidite vaga dona zemay . . . ," recalling Landini's "Vidite." Notation and type of text suggest northern Italy, indicating the extension of Landini's influence into the early fifteenth century.

MODENA, BIBL. ESTENSE, α.M. 5, 24 (olim. lat. 568) (Mod; Est)

   7 by named composers, transcribed
   1 anonymous work, transcribed

This codex in particular exemplifies the change in musical taste, with the introduction of French stylistic and technical elements into Italy. While most of the composers are Italian, the majority of works are in the French style and language.

---

50. Not actually relevant here, though certainly worthy of attention, are the additional fragments containing sacred music recently discovered at Grottaferrata, which Ursula Günther, in her thorough study (*Cert* III [1970], 315–397) designates as *Collocazione provvisoria 197* (Gr).

Apel *3* (1953), 404. (VII)

Besseler *13:1* (1925), 230. (I)

Clercx *4:*I (1960), 71–74. (I)

—— *6* (1959), 111–114. (V a)

Fano *2* (1953), 7–14.

* —— *3* (1956), 109–135. (I)

Ficker *2* (1960), 142.
    In spite of the French influence, there still remains a delight in the
    melisma.

Günther. "Das Manuskript Modena, Biblioteca Estense, α.M.5,24 (olim lat.
    568 = Mod)." *MD* XXIV (1970), 17–67.
    A scholarly investigation into the nature of this manuscript, with inventory
    and concordances. Pp. 48–50 contain lists of manuscript inventories.

Ludwig *1* (1904–05), 616–618. (I)

—— *2* (1928), 30–31.

* Pirrotta *11* (1946), 5–45.

—— *15* (1948), 129. (I)

Wolf *5:*I (1904), 335–339. (I)

Wouters, Jos. *Harmonische Verschijningsvormen in de Muziek van de XIIIe
    tot de XVIe Eeuw.* [Amsterdam? 1954?], 142. (VII)

NEW YORK, PRIVATE LIBRARY OF PROFESSOR EDWARD E. LOWIN-
    SKY, now at Chicago (NYL)

        4 [+1] by Paolo, transcribed
        1 anonymous work [?] transcribed

Fischer *32* (1956), 10, 98, 110. (I)

* Pirrotta *33* (1961). (III a)

OSTIGLIA FRAGMENT, see ROME, BIBL. VATICANA, Rossi 215 (V b)

OXFORD, BODLEIAN LIBRARY, Canonici Misc. 213 (O; O 213)

        20 by named composers, all transcribed

Borren, Charles Van den. "The Codex Canonici 213 in the Bodleian Library
    at Oxford." *PRMA* LXXIII (1946), 45–58.
    A review of Stainer.

—— *6* (1938), 182.

—— *9* (1941), 56. (I)

* Nicholson (1898), vii–xix.

> History and physical description (including the notation and its relation to dates), contents, composers by nationality and location, and remarks pertaining to French and Italian dialects of the poems. A suggestion that the original collections from which the manuscript was copied were made by Dufay.

Reaney. "Bodleian Library . . . Canonici Misc 213 (O) [Oxforder Handschriften]." *MGG* X (1962), 517–518.

* ———— 6 (1970).

> Not only composers, but compositions and scribes were closely connected with Italy. Despite speculations about who wrote the manuscript, the strong feeling is that Italians alone were involved in the copying. Chronology is complex.

————. "The Manuscript Oxford, Bodleian Library Canonici misc. 213." *MD* IX (1955), 73–104.

> Description and origins, composers, tables, concordances, bibliography, inventory. Suggests Venice as the place where it was compiled and stresses Dufay's personal connection with it. Questions the validity of the dates inserted in the manuscript, which range from 1422 to 1436.

* Stainer, Sir John, J. F. R., and C., eds. *Dufay and His Contemporaries*. London and New York, Novello, 1898.

> Pp. 1–45: pertaining to the composers, the songs, notation, *musica ficta* and performance problems. Pp. 199–207: thematic index.[51]

Wolf 2 (1899–1900). (IV)

> A review of Stainer.

Wouters (1954), 87. (VII)

PADUA FRAGMENTS, BIBL. UNIVERSITARIA

MANUSCRIPTS 684 and 1475 (PadA) [Oxford, Bodleian Library, Can. Pat. lat. 229]

> 10 by named composers, 9 transcribed [52]
> 1 anonymous work, transcribed

Besseler *13:1* (1925), 228–230. (I)

> Inventory (including concordances).

Clercx *4:*I (1960), 76. (I)

———— 7 (1956), 156–157. (I)

---

51. Said by Reaney *9* to be insufficient.

52. Included among these are one composition from the Oxford fragment, one by Landini which is unidentified by Besseler, and one by Jacopo which Besseler considers as belonging to PadC (Fischer *32*, 27 n. 100), and which Pirrotta attributes to both PadA and PadC (Pirrotta *26:*IV, iv).

Fischer. "Padua u. Paduaner Handschriften." *MGG* X (1962), 571–572.

——— *32* (1956), 98. (I)

Frati, Ludovico. "Frammento di un codice musicale del secolo XIV." *Giornale storico della letteratura italiana* XVIII (1891), 438–439.

Ludwig *1* (1904–05), 615–616. (I)

——— *2* (1928), 25.

Pirrotta *11* (1946), 37.

Plamenac *2* (1955), 166.

Wolf *5*:I (1904), 258–259. (I)

MANUSCRIPT 1115 (PadB)

2 by named composers, 1 transcribed
1 anonymous work, transcribed

Besseler *13:I* (1925), 231. (I)
Inventory (including concordances).

Clercx *4*:I (1960), 75–76. (I)

——— *7* (1956), 156–157. (I)

Pirrotta *11* (1946), 37 n. 2.
Wolf *5*:I (1904), 259–260. (I)

MANUSCRIPT 658 (PadC)

2 by Jacopo, transcribed

Besseler *13:II* (1926), 233–235. (I)
Inventory (Including concordances).

Clercx *4*:I (1960), 76–77. (I)

Fischer *32* (1956), 97, 102.

Pirrotta *11* (1946), 37, n. 2.

Plamenac *2* (1955), 166 n. 2.

PARIS, BIBL. NATIONALE, nouv. acq. franç. 4917 (Pz; P 49)

4 by named composers, transcribed
4 anonymous works, transcribed

Clercx *4*:I (1960), 79. (I)

Ellinwood *4* (1939), xx.

Fischer *32* (1956), 11, 103. (I)

PERUGIA FRAGMENT, see LUCCA, ARCHIVIO DI STATO (V b)

PISTOIA FRAGMENT, see LUCCA ARCHIVIO DI STATO (V b)

ROME, BIBL. APOSTOLICA VATICANA URBINATE, lat. 1419 (RU₁)

    1 by Donato, transcribed [53]
    1 anonymous work, transcribed

Besseler *13:I* (1925), 226, 227

Fischer *32* (1956), 97, 102. (I)

ROME, BIBL. APOSTOLICA VATICANA URBINATE, lat. 1411 (RU₂)

    2 by named composers, transcribed
    1 anonymous work, transcribed

Besseler *13:I* (1925), 242. (I)

Wolf *5:I* (1904), 192–193. (I)

ROME, BIBL. CASATENENSE, c II, 3 (Cas)

    2 by Ugolino, transcribed
Wolf *5:I* (1904), 339–340. (I)

SEVILLA, BIBL. COLOMBINA, 5 2 25 (Sev)

    1 by Landini, transcribed
Gallo, F. Alberto. "Alcune fonti di musica teorica e pratica." *Cert* II (1968), 59–73.

SIENA FRAGMENTS, ARCHIVIO DI STATO (Sie)

    3 anonymous works, transcribed

Besseler *13:I* (1925), 230 n. 4.

Ghisi *10* (1946), 182. (V b)
    Author does not dismiss the possibility that this first fragment may belong to the Lucca or some other codex.

    ———. "A Second Sienese Fragment of the Italian Ars Nova." *MD* II (1948), 173–177.
    It is pointed out that there is some disparity between the first fragment and this second one, which constitutes an important addition to the music of this period. The two Italian secular compositions here have the same characteristics as those in other fragments at the periphery of the late Ars

---

53. So considered by Marrocco in *6*:VII.

Nova, but these two erotic ballate have thus far not been known to exist elsewhere. This late Ars Nova notation is typical of the period, and the author feels it could belong to the historical and stylistic movement of 1435–1455, represented by later codices.

STRASBOURG, Ms. 222 C. 22 (Str)

2[?] by named composers, transcribed [?] [54]

* Borren 2 (1924).
Following a brief account of the unique history of this manuscript, the author points out that this is not the work of a single copyist, and that the manuscript is international in scope. The wide range of notation styles would indicate that its dates extend from the late fourteenth century to about 1440–1460. Also considered are problems of identification.

* ——— 9 (1941), 53–54. (I)
Characterized as a "transition" manuscript.

* ———. *Le manuscrit musical 222 C. 22 de la bibliothèque de Strasbourg.* . . . Anvers, E. Secelle, 1924. (Extrait des *Annales de l'académie royale d'archéologie de Belgique*, 1923.)
The original manuscript was burned in 1870, but was reconstructed from a partial copy of Edmond de Coussemaker. This is a study of the reconstructed manuscript, with description and alphabetic index by text incipit indicating color of notation. Detailed analysis of each composition. Inventory (including concordances).

Fischer *12* (1957), 43, 45.

Gülke, Peter. "Strassburg, MS. 222 C 22." *MGG* XII (1965), 1437–1438.
". . . perhaps now in the Stiftsbibliothek."

Ludwig *1* (1904), 618. (I)

——— 2 (1928), 37.

Wolf 5:I (1904), 384–389. (I)

PERFORMANCE PRACTICE (VI)

The question of performance practice in the Trecento will always leave room for speculation. With the increasing interest in the recording and live performance of this music, scholars find themselves confronted with challenging questions. In respect to performance, the upper voice remains an invariable, with its melismatic quality, so characteristically Italian. But the other voices lend themselves to a wide range of possibilities. It is not to be denied that they

---

54. These are Nucella's "De bon parole" and Anthonius' (or Zacara's?) "E ardo in un fugo," and will probably appear in Marrocco *6*;X.

too could be sung, even though they are at times without text. Schering's theory (Schering *4, 5*) has now been virtually discarded, and the study of fourteenth-century iconography and literature has resulted in an extensive amplification of Riemann's theory (Riemann *1*).

Becherini *2* (1962).
> A further pursuance of the observations of Riemann, Wolf, Ludwig, and Schering regarding the use of instruments, with particular reference to the *Decamerone* and *Il Paradiso degli Alberti.*

Bonaccorsi *2* (1948). (I)

Bonaventura *1* (1914).
> An examination of the *Decamerone* reveals that the spontaneous and simple music that flourished in the Trecento was often accompanied on viols, lute, and guitar.

Bonaventura *2* (1904), Chapter IV. (I)

Borren *5* (1940).
> The first examination of the contents of the Codex Faenza 117, in which the author suggests that some of the figurations were intended to be performed as a pizzicato. Notes that in some cases the music was intended for two instruments.

————. "Dufay and his School." *NOH* (1960), 226.

Cellesi (1927–28).
> Regarding performance, performers, and the instruments used.

Dart, Thurston. *The Interpretation of Music.* 4th ed. London, Hutchinson, 1960, 147–172.
> "Interspersed instruments" might well include glockenspiel, bassoon, drum, and other instruments.

Fano *3* (1956), 66–67. (I)

Fischer, Kurt von. "A propos de la répartition du texte et le nombre de voix dans les oeuvres italiennes du Trecento." *Wég* (1959), 232–238.
> A discussion based on Fischer *32.*

Ghisi. "An Angel Concert in a Trecento Sienese Fresco." *ReeFest* (1966), 308–313.
> This article, as well as Ghisi *2* and *7*, points out that the iconography of this period can provide reliable clues to performance practice.

———— *2* (1968). (I)

———— *7* (1970). (I)

Göllner, Theodor. "Die Trecento-Notation und der Tactus in der ältesten deutschen Orgelquellen." *Cert* III (1970), 176–185.

Greenberg, Noah. "Early Music Performance Today." *ReeFest* (1966), 314–318.

Gullo, Salvatore. *Das Tempo in der Musik des XIII. und XIV. Jahrhundert.* Bern, Paul Haupt, 1964. (Schweizerischen musikforschenden Gesellschaft.)

The question is posed: What possibility was afforded to musicians of the thirteenth and fourteenth centuries to determine tempo in a given piece?

Gutmann (1928–29).

Haas, Robt. *Aufführungspraxis der Musik.* Potsdam, Athenaion, 1931, 93–100.

Handschin 2 (1931), 26–27. (I)
In practice, musicians probably sang only the upper voice of the madrigal, because of its coloratura quality, and played the lower voice on an instrument.

Harrison (1966). (I)
Cites evidence that the lute was used only for dancing. Perhaps the organ was principally a solo instrument. Appropriate to this music are the five-string fiddle, harp, psaltry, cittern, and large transverse flute.

Ludwig 4 (1902–03), 46–66. (I)

Marrocco 6:VI (1967).
P. xii: suggestions for performance. P. 172: to the effect that five of the keyboard compositions in Faenza are on tenors taken from Jacopo by an anonymous late fourteenth-century arranger.

Pirrotta. "Note su un codice di antiche musiche per tastiera." *RMI* LVI (1954), 333–339.
Regarding Faenza and instrumental versions.

Plamenac 1 (1970).

Plamenac 3 (1954).
Faenza Codex.

———— 4 (1964).

———— 5 (1951).
The repertory of this codex (formerly called the *Bonadies Codex*) is thought to have been intended primarily for performance on a keyboard instrument, though this view does not agree with those of Van den Borren and Jeppeson, namely, that the notation on each staff of a two-staff score was intended for basically monophonic instruments. Plamenac feels this was to be performed on a polyphonic solo instrument, for otherwise notation in two separate parts would have been employed.

———— 6 (1952).

Reaney 12 (1970), 55. (I)

————. "The Performance of Medieval Music." *ReeFest* (1966), 704–722.
In Italy, the general basic structure of Trecento composition was the two-part madrigal, or vocal duet. Even with the appearance of the three-part ballata of Landini, the two-part texture continued to predominate. Instruments could double or ornament, and the organ very likely played an ornamented version of the vocal duet. Instruments therefore played a secondary role, with the possible exception of Codex Faenza.

Riemann *1* (1905), 305–335. (I)

Advances the theory that instruments were interspersed with the voice.

Sachs (1953), 32–34. (I)

Concerning some problems of tempo.

Schering, Arnold. *Aufführungspraxis alter Musik*. Leipzig, Quelle & Meyer, 1931, 16–18.

———— "Das kolorierte Orgelmadrigal des Trecento." *SIMG* XIII (1911–12), 172–204.

Challenges Riemann's theory that stringed instruments were interspersed with voice (see above). Prefers theory that these compositions were performed entirely on the organ. This theory has since been refuted. In connection with this, see musical supplement of this article, which has not been included in this bibliography.

———— *5* (1913 [14?]), 54–67. (I)

Stainer (1898), 19–26.

Wolf *8* (1931). (I)

Remarks on Trecento performance practices, which were "as variable . . . as our own," and concerning which no complete description can be found. Nevertheless, it is certain that perfect performance demanded cooperation of voices and instruments.

———— *12* (1938), 63. (II)

Speculation regarding the extent to which instruments were used.

TRECENTO THEORY (INCLUDING NOTATION) AND RELATED TREATISES (VII)

No study of any given period in music history can ignore the area of theory; this statement is singularly true of the study of the fourteenth century, since theoretical treatises are closely linked with the new practice of mensural notation. Reflecting an increasing awareness of this fourteenth-century theory, present-day researches have brought to light a number of hitherto unknown Trecento treatises. Although this guide does not purport to provide a comprehensive bibliography of literature pertaining to the treatises, it is nevertheless hoped that the entries contained in the following section will serve as a useful contribution to a study of the entire Trecento period. The treatises themselves are listed in Appendix III.

Apel *3* (1953).

Deals with origins and principles of Italian notation, with examples in facsimile from Pit, PR, and Rs. This latter is a link between the Petronian and the fully developed Italian system. Mannered notation and mixed notation are considered.

Besseler, Heinrich. "Johannes de Muris." *MGG* VII (1958), 105–111.

Bragard, Roger. "Le *Speculum musicae* du compilateur Jacques de Liège." *MD* VII (1953), 59–104; VIII (1954), 1–17.

Carapetyan *1* (1957). (I)
A lengthy exposition of this treatise in the Tuscan dialect, now kept in the Biblioteca Laurenziana. An elementary text of mensural instruction in the vernacular, dating from about the latter part of the fourteenth century, this is one of three surviving treatises of Florentine origin, the others being Jacopo's *Arte del biscanto misurato* ("rather inconsequential") and Paolo's *Ars ad adiscendum contrapunctum*. . . . It is suspected that other treatises of that period have been lost. The treatise is on pp. 36–57.

———. "A Fourteenth-Century Florentine Treatise in the Vernacular." *MD* IV:1 (1950), 81–92.
A study of the anonymous treatise, *Notitia del valore delle note del canto misurato*. Observations made here are similar to those contained in the citation above, published seven years later.

Clercx, Suzanne. "Les accidents sous-entendus et la transcription en notation moderne." *Wég* (1959), 167–195.
With particular reference to problems of transcription: modern bar lines; implied accidentals in particular.

——— *4*:I (1960), Chapter III. (I)

———. "Le traité *De musica* de Georges Anselme de Parme." *RB* XV (1961), 161–167.
A discussion of a little known fourteenth-century treatise which is in the form of a dialogue between Georgius Anselmus of Parma and Petrus dei Rossi of Parma, dealing with various aspects of music. Treatise links the art of singing with time values which are indicated by measured notation.

Fano *3* (1956), 28–30. (I)

Favaro, Antonio. *Intorno alla vita e alle opere di Prosdocimus*. . . . Roma, 1879. (*Bolletino di bibliografia e di storia delle scienze matematiche e fisiche*. Jan.–Apr., 1879.)

Fischer *11* (1959).
A discussion provoked by Fischer *32* reveals a variety of viewpoints regarding the significance of notation styles in Trecento manuscripts.

——— *32* (1956), 111–123. (I)
Every aspect of notation is considered, from the standpoints of theory, as indicated in the contemporary treatises, and practice, as manifested in the manuscripts themselves. In regard to the latter, it is pointed out that the discrepancies between different versions of the same composition are the inevitable result of the wide dissemination of the manuscripts. Emphasis is placed on the composer's own notation *versus* those of the various scribes, all of which is linked with the time and place of the compilation of each manuscript.

————. "Zur Entwicklung der italienischen Trecento-Notation." *AfMW* XVI (1959), 87–99.

A reply to Reaney's review of Fischer *32* (Reaney *15*) regarding Trecento notation. An analysis and clarification of notation styles in various manuscripts, with reference to some specific compositions.

Gallo, F. Alberto. *Mensurabilis Musicae Tractatuli.* Bologna, 1966. (*Antiquae Musicae Italicae Scriptores,* 1.)

A collection of eight treatises, running the gamut of the fourteenth century, documenting the historical evolution of notation in Italy.

————. *La teoria della notazione in Italia dalla fine del XIII all'inizio del XV secolo.* Bologna, Tamari, 1966. (*Antiquae Musicae Italicae Subsidia Theorica,* 2.)

A survey of the treatises relative to notation in Italy from the end of the Duecento to the beginning of the Quattrocento, set in historical perspective. This preliminary research is intended to facilitate a study of the various gaps yet to be filled in. Bibliographical footnotes.

————. "La tradizione dei trattati musicali di Prosdocimo de Beldemandis." *Quadrivium* VI (1964), 57–82.

Gasperini (1913), 613 ff.

Gennrich, Friedrich. *Abriss der Mensuralnotation des XIV und der ersten Hälfte des XV Jahrhunderts.* Nieder-Modau, 1948. (*Musikwissenschaftliche Studienbibliothek,* 3–4), 5–31.

Göllner 2 (1970). (VI)

Günther 7 (1962–63).

The practice of mensural notation is demonstrated by means of the compositions themselves, since they are more reliable and convincing than theoretical treatises. The positions taken by Wolf and Van that Italy must have introduced the binaria into France are held as untenable; and it is agreed with Besseler, Handschin, and Reaney that there had been evidence of duple rhythms in France even before the fourteenth century.

Gushee, Lawrence. "New Sources for the Biography of Johannes de Muris." *JAMS* XXII (1969), 3–26.

Haberl, Franz X. "Bio-bibliographische Notizen über Ugolino von Orvieto." *KJ* Ser. 2, X (1895), 40–49.

Harman (1958), 154–155, 167. (I)

Special mention of the mixed notation characteristic of Italy, of the "Landini sixth cadence" (termed misleading), and of *musica ficta.*

Hüschen, Heinrich. "Beldemandis." *MGG* I (1949), 1575–1579.

————. "Jacobus von Lüttich (Jacobus de Leodio . . . Jacques de Liège)." *MGG* VI (1957), 1626–1631.

————. "Marchettus von Padua." *MGG* VIII (1960), 1626–1629.

Kornmüller, Utto. "Musiklehre des Ugolino von Orvieto." *KJ*, Ser. 2, X (1895), 19–40.

Kühn, Hellmut. "Das Problem der Harmonik in der Musik der Ars Nova." Doctoral dissertation (unpublished?), Saarbrucken, 1970.

Ludwig *1* (1904–05), 600–607. (I)

Marrocco *7* (1954), 25–27. (II)

Martinez *1* (1964). (I)

———. "Marchettus of Padua and Chromaticism." *Cert* III (1970), 187–202.

* ——— *3* (1963). (I)

Nicholson (1898), ix–x. (IV)

Parrish, Carl. *The Notation of Medieval Music*. New York, W. W. Norton, 1957, 166–182.
> A clear analysis of the system of *divisiones*, with a concise explanation of some transcription techniques.

Reaney. "The *Ars Nova* of Philippe de Vitry." *MD* X (1956), 5–33.[55]

Sachs (1953). (I)
> "Tempo": pp. 32–34. "Later Middle Ages": pp. 179–197 (notation in particular); French *versus* Italian.

* Sartori, Claudio. *La notazione italiana del Trecento*. Firenze, Olschki, 1938.
> This deals chiefly with Prosdocimo de Beldemandis and the Italian secular music of the Trecento. To Prosdocimo's own expositions of his "Tractatus practice cantus mensurabilis ad modum Italicorum" are added Sartori's observations, in which he refers to the "Tractatus" as the principal source that served Johannes Wolf in his studies of Italian notation. Examples of measured notation, and some remarks on the relationship between the Prosdocimus treatise and Marchettus' *Pomerium*. The treatise is on pp. 35–71.

Seay, Albert. "The *Declaratio musice discipline* of Ugolino of Orvieto: Addenda." *MD* XI (1957), 126–133.
> This is actually a continuation of the study in *MD* IX (below), with descriptions of four newly discovered manuscripts of the *Declaratio*. . . . A quotation on p. 128 refers to "other compositions" of Ugolino and leads to some speculation regarding the nature of these compositions.

———. "Paolo da Firenze: A Trecento Theorist." *Cert* I (1962), 118–140.
> This is concerned principally with Paolo's treatise, but there are remarks on a number of other contemporary treatises.

———. "Ugolino da Orvieto." *EM* IV (1964), 444.

---

55. Relevant to this study because the question of the Vitry treatise vis à vis Marchettus' *Pomerium* arises frequently. Page 5 points out (as does Besseler *1*) the principal fourteenth-century sources in which occur the words "Ars Nova."

———. "Ugolino of Orvieto, theorist and composer." *MD* IX (1955), 111–166.

———. "Ugolino von Orvieto." *MGG* XIII (1966), 1022–1023.

* Smith, F. Joseph. *Iacobi Leodiensis "Speculum musicae": A Commentary.* 2 vols. Brooklyn, Institute of Mediaeval Music, 1966–69. (*Musicological Studies,* 13, 22).

A scholarly investigation into what the author considers "perhaps the crowning work of musical theory in the Middle Ages," providing as it does "an encyclopedic grasp of mediaeval music theory." This study is confined to the first five books of the encyclopedic *Speculum.* A comprehensive bibliography is provided.

Stainer (1898), 30–35. (V c)
Regarding Dufay's modulations, and *musica ficta.*

\# Steiner (1931).

Stellfeld, Bent. "Prosdocimus de Beldemandis als Erneuerer der Musikbetrachtung um 1400." In *Natalica musicologica Knud Jeppesen,* ed. by Bjorn Hjelmborg and Søren Sørensen. Hafnia, W. Hansen, 1962, 37–50.

* Strunk *1* (1950). (I)
Regarding the chronology of the Vitry and Marchettus treatises. Conclusion is that *Pomerium* was written in April 1319 as the probable *latest* date. Regardless of other debts to France, the first Trecentists depended in no way upon Johannes de Muris or Vitry. Marchettus with his *Lucidarium* (plainsong) and *Pomerium* (mensural notation) was the principal spokesman for the Italian Trecento.

———, ed. *Source Readings in Music History: Antiquity and the Middle Ages.* New York, Norton, 1950, 139–190.
Jacobus de Liège is now recognized as the author of the *Speculum musicae,* formerly thought to be by Johannes de Muris.

Toguchi *1* (1963).

Vecchi, Giuseppe. *Su la composizione del "Pomerium" di Marchetto da Padova e la "Brevis compilatio."* Bologna, 1957. (*Quadrivium, s.m.,* 1.)
An assessment of the *Pomerium,* its scope and the cultural climate in which it was written. It is pointed out that the *Pomerium* provides a panorama of the mensural practices of that period and does not suggest innovations. There are also some observations on the *Brevis compilatio.*

Wolf, Johannes. "L'arte del biscanto misurato secondo il maestro Jacopo da Bologna." In *Theodor Kroyer Festschrift.* Regensburg, G. Bosse, 1933, 17–39.

——— 2 (1899–1900), 157–162. (I)

——— 4 (1901–02), 603–605. (I)

——— 5:I (1904), 215–356. (I)

————. *Handbuch der Notationskunde.* Vol. I. Leipzig, Breitkopf & Härtel, 1913, 287–239.

————. "La notazione italiana nel secolo XIV." *NM* II:4 (Oct. 1899), 73–75.

Wouters (1954), 62–78, 87, 123–129, 141–142.
> Emphasis is on the harmonic development, as found particularly in the cadence, with examples. The importance of the "Landini cadence": pp. 64–78.

Transcriptions

WORKS BY KNOWN COMPOSERS (VIII a) [56]

From the following entries it will be observed that within the past several years extended researches have yielded additional information on some composers, notably Bartolino and Paolo. Furthermore, the works of hitherto neglected composers have been transcribed for the first time. Yet for numerous Tercento composers, little if any biographical information is available. Whenever possible, the composer's name and dates are followed by (1) a roman numeral indicating the generation to which he most nearly belongs; [57] (2) the scene of his activity; (3) original sources containing his works; and (4) his total number of works, followed by the number of those transcribed. If there are several sources, the principal ones are italicized. As in the Manuscript Sources sections, questionable data are so indicated with either brackets or a question mark, or both.

Section A lists the composer's works in transcription. In cases where there is a complete edition or where a substantial number of works is found in a single collection, these are cited first. Sources containing other transcriptions follow in alphabetical order. A complete edition is indicated by an asterisk (*).

Section B lists literature relating to the composer and to his works.

1. ANDREA DEI SERVI (FRATER ANDREAS ORGANISTA DE FLOR-
ENTIA; FRA ANDREA DI GIOVANNI), d. *ca.* 1415; II [or III?]; Florence
and Pistoia; *Sq*, Lo, Pit; 30 [+1?] works, 30 transcribed.

---

56. By "known" is meant through concordances, though, as has been pointed out, there are occasionally some questions of attribution.

57. See p. 2, above.

A

* Marrocco *6:*X; 30 works.
* Pirrotta *26:*V; nos. 1–30.

WolfSq, 335–359; 29 works.
Marrocco *3;* no. 8.[58]

B

Ellinwood *1* (1960), 80–81.
Ghisi *3* (1962), 52, 53.
——— *9* (1938), 167.
——— *14* (1962), 37–38.
Königslöw (1940), 34–35.
LiGotti *5* (1944), 91, 96–100.
Pirrotta 26:V (1964), i–ii.
Reaney *1* (1960), 301.
——— *12* (1970), 59.

Taucci, 34, 35, 37, 38; 4 works.
Wolf. "Musica fiorentina nel secolo

XIV." *NM,* Supplement II, 72,
214, 215; 3 works.

Taucci (1935).
A study of the life and work of
Andrea, with speculation that Sq
may have been written by his hand.
Four ballate, transcribed by Pir-
rotta.
WolfSq (1955), Introduction, ix.

2. ANDREA STEFANI (STEPHANI), 2d half of fourteenth century; II [or
III?]; Florence and Lucca; Luc; 3 works, transcribed.

A

* Marrocco *6:*X; 3 works.
* Pirrotta *26:*V; nos. 41–43.
——— *10:*II, 152.

B

Bonaccorsi, Alfredo. "A. Stefani, musicista dell'Ars Nova." *RaM* XVIII
    (1948), 103–105.
    Author considers Stefani important, though points out that he was
    neither poet nor musician by profession. Mentions three works in
    Lucca Codex.
——— *2* (1948), 596–597.
Ghisi *16* (1953), 48.
LiGotti. "Per la biografia di due minori musicisti italiani dell'Ars Nova."
——— *8* (1947), 98–105.
Mancini (1947), 90–91.
Pirrotta *10:II* (1950), 149.
——— *10:III* (1951), 140–141.
——— *26:*V (1964), iii.

---

58. Published in the first edition as anonymous.

3. ANTONELLO (MAROT) (ANTONELLUS AMAROTUS), ABBAS DE (DA) CASERTA, late fourteenth and early fifteenth centuries; III; vicinity of Naples; Luc, PadB, Parma, Str; 7 [+1?] works, all transcribed.

A

Marrocco *6:*X; 7 works.
Disertori, Benvenuto. *La frottola nella storia della musica.* Cremona, Athenaeum cremonense, 1954. (Extract from *Instituta e monumenta*, Ser. 1, I), xii.[59]

B

Apel *1* (1950), 1, 4, 8.
Bonaccorsi 2 (1948), 590–594.
    Includes remarks on the various forms of the name.
Borren 2 (1924), 530.
Disertori (1954), xii.
Fano *3* (1956), 41, 64, 65.
Ficker 2 (1960), 142.
Ghisi *10* (1946), 184.

Gombosi (1950), 604.
Korte 2 (1933), 77.
Mancini (1947), 89.
Pirrotta *10:III* (1951), 133–135.
———— *11* (1946), 36.
———— *37* (1953), 12, 13, 16–17.
Reaney *1* (1960), 302.
ReeR (1959), 31, 33.

4. ANTONIUS CLERICUS APOSTOLICUS;[60] Str; 1 work, transcribed.[61]

A

Marrocco *6:*X.

5. ANTONIUS ROMANUS (ANTONIO ROMANO); Padua (?) and Venice (1415–1425); O; 1 work, transcribed.

A

Gallo, ed. Antonii Romani. *Opera.* Bologna, 1965; no. 7.
Marrocco *6:*X.

B

Clercx *4:*I (1960), 69.
Gallo. "Antonius Romanus." *MGG*, supp. I (1970?), 239–240.
Reaney *6* (1970), 447, 452.

---

59. Fischer lists this as anonymous (Fischer *32*), and states that it has been erroneously ascribed to Antonellus (Fischer *33*, 199). Bonaccorsi supports Disertori's view (Bonaccorsi 2, 593).

60. Perhaps Antonio Zacara? (Fischer *32*, 50, n. 238.)

61. Forthcoming. This ballata, "E, ardo in un fugo," is a unicum, and almost illegible. Dr. Marrocco states that it has presented transcription problems.

6. ARRIGO (HENRICUS), late fourteenth century [?]; Pit, PR; 1 work, transcribed.

A

Marrocco 6:X.
Wolf 5:III; no. 57 (a and b).

B

Fischer *15* (1957), 41.
Reaney *10* (1960), 39.
Wolf 5:I (1904), 251.

7. BARTOLINO (BARTOLINUS) DA PADUA (MAGISTER FRATER BARTOLUS DE . . . ; FRATER CARMELITUS; DACTALUS), *fl.* 1380–1410; III; [62] north Italian Ars Nova, perhaps Venice in addition to Padua; *Sq*, PR (here anon.), Mod, Lo, Luc, Pit (here Scapuccia); 38 works, all transcribed.

A

* Marrocco 6:IX; 38 works.
WolfSq, 159–194; 36 works.
Fischer 7, 277.[63]
Wolf 5:III; nos. 43–46.

B

Bonaccorsi 2 (1948), 582–584.
Borren, Charles Van den. "Actions et réactions de la polyphonie néerlandaise et la polyphonie italienne. . . ." *Revue belge d'archéologie et d'histoire de l'art* VI:1 (1936), 52 n. 1.
    Regarding a ballata as a basis for a polyphonic lauda.
Clercx 7 (1956), 155.
Ellinwood *1* (1960), 76.
    Feels that Bartolino is wrongly identified with Bartholus de Florentia.
Fischer 7 (1958–61), 277–281.
    Author, through a stylistic analysis of this unicum in PR, submits evidence that it is by Bartolino.
Ghisi. "Bartolino da Padua." *MGG* I (1949), 1349–1350.
——— *10* (1946), 178–179, 183–184.
Goldine, Nicole. "Fra Bartolino da Padova, musicien de cour." *Acta* XXXIV (1962), 142–155.
    A paper read at Wégimont in 1962, by means of sphragistics and numismatics connects him with the Carrara family and speculates that

---

62. Petrobelli is inclined to place him in II, with Landini's generation.
63. This appears as an anonymous work in Marrocco *3*.

he was perhaps a poet-musician at court. His work reflects a refinement
of taste, and the political character of numerous texts is conspicuous.
Königslöw (1940), 19–20.

LiGotti 5 (1944), 87–90.

Petrobelli, Pierluigi. "Some Dates for Bartolino da Padova." In *Studies in
Music History: Essays for Oliver Strunk,* ed. by Harold Powers. Princeton, 1968, 94–112.

> Regarding heraldic allusions in texts; allusions to people and to his-
> torical events. Here again the application of sphragistics and nu-
> mismatics has yielded additional information, and this device is recom-
> mended as a means of relating the lives of individual composers to
> the social milieu in which they worked.

Pirrotta. "Bartolino da Padova." *EM* I (1963), 196.

——— *10:III* (1951), 119–122.

——— *11* (1946), 28.

8. BARTOLOMEO (BARTOLOMEUS) DE BONONIA (BOLOGNA), late
fourteenth and early fifteenth centuries; III; Benedictine monk, likely from
the north; O, PR; 2 works, transcribed.

A

Marrocco *6:X*; 2 works.
Stainer, 60.

B

Borren. "Dufay and His School."
 NOH (1960), 225.
——— *9* (1941), 121.
Fischer *12* (1957), 47–50.
Pirrotta. "Bartolomeo de Bono-
nia." *EM* I (1963), 196.
Reaney *1* (1960), 302.
——— *6* (1970), 453–454.
——— *12* (1970), 60–61.
ReeR (1959), 26, 28.

9. BIANCHY (BIANCHUS), JACOBELUS [?]; PR; 2 works, transcribed.

A

Marrocco *6:X*; 2 works.
Wolf *5:III*; no. 58.

B

Wolf *5:I* (1904), 285.

BONAIUTO CORSINI, see CORSINI

BRISIENSIS, see MATTEO DA BRESCIA

10. BROLLO, BARTOLOMEO (DE BROLIS; DE BRUDIS; also BROLO, BRUOLO, BRUOLLIS, B. TREBOLIS), *fl.* 1400–1420; III; Venice; O;

3 [?] works, transcribed.[64]

A

Marrocco *6*:X.
BorrenPS, 293.[65]

B

Borren *7* (1914), 17–19.
Reaney *6* (1970), 451–452.
———— *9* (1955), 79.
ReeR (1959), 26.

CASERTA, see ANTONELLO

11. CICONIA, JOHANNES, *ca.* 1335–1411; III; born in Liège, but in close contact with Italian Ars Nova; in Padua, 1402–1411; *Luc* (fragments of work found in Dom, PadB, Parma, PC, Pit, Pz, RU$_2$, Str.); 14 [+2] works, 14 transcribed.

A

Clercx *4*:II, 43–75; 14 works.[66]
Marrocco *6*:X; 12 works.
DTO VII, 227.
Fano *3*, 392.[67]
Ghisi *5*, 35.
————, ed. "Italian Ars Nova Music. . . ." *JRB* I:4 (1946). (Musical supplement to Ghisi *10*), 2, 3, 5, 6, 10, 11, 21, 23; 9 works.[68]
Riemann *2*, II: 1, 89.

---

64. Wrote mainly chansons in the French style (ReeR, 26). Is "Vivere et recte riminiscere" his only true Italian ballata?
65. The only secular work in BorrenPS, with partially Latinized text.
66. Although these constitute the Italian part of a complete edition, there remains at least one of his known Italian works yet unpublished, "Amor per te sempre," which the editor states could not be transcribed since it was found to be partly illegible (Clercx *4*:II, 13).
67. Here is included a contratenor by Matheus d[e] P[erusi]o.
68. Those on pp. 2, 11, and 21 are for *one* voice only.

Wolf *5*:III; no. 30.

B

Besseler. "Ciconia, Johannes." *MGG* II (1952), 1423–1434.
Bonaccorsi *2* (1948), 585–588.
Borren *6* (1938), 179–180.
———— *8* (1960), 225.
———— *9* (1941), 28–29.
Bukofzer (1948), 168, 170–171.
Clercx. "Ciconia, Johannes." *EM* I (1963), 480–481.
———— *4*:I (1960), 20–27, 41–45, 82–86.
    Special reference to Italy.
————. "Johannes Ciconia de Leodio." *RIMS* (Utrecht, 1952), 107–126.
———— *6* (1959).
Fano *3* (1956), 65–66.
———— *4* (1962), 107, 111.
Fischer *12* (1957), 46.
———— *27* (1963), 76.
    To the effect that the Reina Codex contains no piece by Ciconia.
———— *36* (1961).
Ghisi *5* (1942), 25–27.
———— *8* (1942), 86–91, 94.[69]
    The Italian version of Ghisi *5*.
———— *10* (1946), 183–184.
Korte *2* (1933), 67.
Krohn, Ernst C. "*Nova musica* of Johannes Ciconia." *Manuscripta* V:1
    (Feb. 1961), 3–16.
    Although this deals with the treatise,[70] considerable space is also
    devoted to the importance of Ciconia as a composer. Bibliography.
Ludwig *1* (1904–05), 639.
Pirrotta *10:III* (1951), 122–133.
Reaney *1* (1960), 297, 301.
———— *12* (1970), 61.
ReeR (1959), 25–30.
Schrade *1* (1959), 48–49.
Wouters (1954), 87.

12. CORSINI, BONAIUTO (PITOR), fourteenth century; Florence; *Lo,* Luc;
    4 works, transcribed.

A

    * Marrocco *6*:X; 4 works.
    * Pirrotta *26*:V; nos. 37–40.

---

69. See also Ghisi's remarks on "Leggiadra donna" in *Liber Amicorum Charles Van den Borren* (Anvers, 1964), 173 ff.

70. For more on Ciconia as a theorist, see Clercx. "Johannes Ciconia, théoricien." *AM* III (1955), 39–75.

Wolf 5:III; no. 59.

B

Bonaccorsi 2 (1948), 614.
Fischer 32 (1956), 9.
LiGotti 3 (1947), 103–105.
    To the effect that he was a poet also and may have supplied his own
    texts.
Pirrotta 26:V (1964), iii.
Reaney 7 (1958), 71.
WolfSq (1955), Introduction, ix.

13. DOMENICO (DOMENICUS) DE FERARIA (FERRARIA), early fifteenth
    century; III [?]; O; 1 work, transcribed.

A

Marrocco 6:X.
Stainer, 160.[71]

B

Reaney 6 (1970), 454.
―――― 9 (1955), 78, 103.

14. DONATO DA FIRENZE (DONATUS DE FLORENTIA; DA CASCIA),
    fourteenth century; Benedictine monk; II [or III?] Florence and Verona
    [?]; *Sq*, FP, Pit, Lo, RU₁; 16 [+1?] works, all transcribed.[72]

A

*   Marrocco 6:VII, 30–72; 17 works.   Wolf 4, 636.
*   Pirrotta 26:III; nos. 18–33.   ―――― 5:III; no. 47.
    WolfSq, 99–116; 15 works.   ―――― 10:II, 71.
    Marrocco 3; no. 11.

B

Casimiri, Rafaello. "Giovanni da   Ludwig 1 (1904–05), 636.
    Cascia e Donato da Cascia mu-   Marrocco 6:VII (1971), Introduc-
    sicisti umbri?" *NA* XI (1934),   tion.
    207–210.   Pirrotta. "Donatus de Florentia
Clercx 7 (1956), 155.   (Dominus)." *MGG* III (1954),
Corsi 2 (1959), 81.   660–661.
Ghisi 3 (1962), 52.   ―――― 26:III (1962), ii.
Königslöw (1940), 15–16.   Reaney 10 (1960), 39.
LiGotti 5 (1944), 71–72.

---

71. Said by Reese (ReeR, 30) to be incorrectly transcribed.
72. The seventeenth work is a virelai, "Je port amiablement," in three different
versions in Marrocco 6:VII.

15. DUFAY, GUILLAUME, ca. 1400–1474. Rimini and Pesaro, 1420–26; Rome, 1428–33, 1435–36; Bologna, 1436–1443. Also Mantova, Assisi, Siena. *O*, RU₂ [?], BU, FP. Only 4 in Italian style, all transcribed.[73]

A

Besseler, ed. *Guillelmi Dufay: Opera Omnia,* Vol. VI. Rome, American Institute of Musicology, 1964 (*CMM*, 1), nos. 1–4.
Marrocco *6*:X; 4 works.

B

Besseler, "Dufay." *MGG* III (1954), 889–912.
———. "Dufay in Rom." *AfMW* XV (1958), 1–19.
——— 7 (1964), i–xiv, xxiv–xxvii.
———. "Neue Dokumente zum Leben und Schaffen Dufays." *AfMW* IX (1951), 166.
Regarding his relations with the Ferrara court.
Borren. "Dufay and His School." *NOH* (1960), 214–217, 225.
——— 9 (1941), 30–47.
P. 34: a conclusion that the years 1420–1425 served as an apprenticeship to the use of the Italian language.
———. *Guillaume Dufay.* . . . Bruxelles, M. Hayez, 1925.
———. "Guillaume Dufay, centre du rayonnement de la polyphonie européenne à la fin du moyen-âge." *Bulletin de l'institut historique belge* XX (1939), 171–185.
Regarding a "new Ars Nova"; Dufay's connections with the Medici and with the papal chapel; his feeling for the Italian language and for Italian polyphony from his adolescent years.
———. "A Light of the Fifteenth Century: Guillaume Dufay." *MQ* XXI (1935), 279–297.
Concerning the Italian texts.
Frati *2* (1924), 61.
Haberl, Franz X. "Wilhelm Dufay." *VfMW* I (1885), 397–530.
Very comprehensive coverage for its day, but now requires much supplementation.
Hamm, Charles E. *A Chronology of the Works of Guillaume Dufay Based on a Study of Mensural Practice.* Princeton, 1964.
Little attention is given to the Italian works.
Nicholson (1898), xvi–xix.
Pirro, André. *Histoire de la musique de la fin du XIVᵉ siècle à la fin du XVIᵉ.* Paris, Librairie Renouard, 1940, 54–87.
P. 64: the years in Rome. Pp. 81, 83: the Italian pieces.
Pirrotta *30* (1966), 678–680.

---

73. Stainer refers to "the six Italian songs," while Besseler *5* lists seven. Haberl names still another, "Merce ti chiamo." But these are not in the Italian style.

Reaney *6* (1970), 457, 461–463.
ReeR (1959), 48–86.
    Pp. 52–53: Italian.
Stainer (1898), 2–11.
    Regarding the "six Italian songs."
Wolff, Hellmuth C. "Dufay, Guillaume." *EM* II (1963), 99–100.

16. EGIDIO DI FRANCIA (DE MURINO; MAGISTER FRATER EGIDIUS; EGIDIUS DE AURELIANIS), fourteenth century; II; Augustinian monk at Santo Spirito; *Sq*, Pit; 5 [?] works, transcribed.

"M. Frater Egidius et Guilelmus de Francia" (Sq). These two names often appear together. There still remains considerable speculation regarding the relationship between these Augustinian monks, who were probably Italianized Frenchmen. Gombosi suspects that they were collaborators. Perhaps the most satisfactory observations to date on the enigma of these two figures come from Dr. Pirrotta (Pirrotta *26:*V, ii). It will be noted that he chooses to attribute the five ballate in Sq as well as the setting of the Sacchetti madrigal, "La neve . . ." (this latter unequivocally by Guilelmus), to Guilelmus, while Prof. Marrocco (Marrocco *6:*IX) attributes three ballate to each composer.

A

    * WolfSq, 319–321; 5 works.
    Marrocco *6:*IX; 3 works.

B

    Carducci *2* (1929) 309.
    Fischer *32* (1965), 8, 25 n. 86.
    Ghisi *3* (1962), 52.
    ——— *14* (1962), 38.
    Gombosi (1950), 604.
    Günther. "Datierbare Balladen des späten 14. Jahrhunderts." *MD* XVI
        (1962), 151 n. 31.
    ———. "Zur Biographie einiger Komponisten ders *Ars subtilior*." *AfMW*
        XXI (1964), 178.
    Hoppin, R. H. and S. Clercx, "Notes biographiques sur quelques musiciens
        français du XIVe siècle." *Wég* (1959), 67, 84, 88, 90–91.
    LiGotti *5* (1944), 66 n. 101.
    Reaney. "Egidius de Murino (de Morino, de Muris, de Mori)." *MGG* III
        (1954), 1169–1172.[74]
    ——— *12* (1970), 60.

---

74. See also Reaney. "The Ms. Chantilly, Musée Condé 1047." *MD* VIII (1954),
68–69.

17. FEO (SER FEO; MAESTRO FEO); *Sq,* Pit; 2 works, transcribed.

A

* Marrocco *6:*X; 2 works.
Pirrotta *26:*V; nos. 44, 45.

B

Pirrotta *26:*V (1964), iii.
"No biographical information; a name only."
Reaney *10* (1960), 39.

18. FR[ANCISCUS] REYNALDUS; Ber; 1 work, transcribed.

A

Fischer *3,* 40.
Marrocco *6:*X.

B

Fischer *3* (1968), 39–40.
   Regarding this hitherto unknown ballata, "L'adorno viso," which he
   dates *ca.* 1400 and which he discovered in a new source (see above).
——— *17* (1964), 83.
Reaney. "Franciscus." *MGG* II (1952), 634–636.

19. GHERARDELLO DA FIRENZE (GHERARDELLUS DE FLORENTIA), d.
   ca 1362–1364; II (I?); Florence; *Sq,* Pit, Lo; 16 works, all transcribed.

A

* Marrocco *6:*VII, 75–117; 16 works.
* Pirrotta *26:*I; nos. 23–38: 16.
* WolfSq, 47–62; 16 works.
CorteSc; no. 26.
GleE, 100.
HAM; no. 52.

Levi, Eugenia. *Lirica italiana an-
   tica.* Firenze, Olschki, 1905, 274b.
Marrocco *3;* no. 25.
Riemann *2,* I:2, 324.
Wolf *4,* 626.
——— *10:*II, 73.

B

Ellinwood *1* (1960), 76.
Königslöw (1940), 16–17.
LiGotti *5* (1944), 68–69.
Pirrotta. "Gherardellus de Floren-
   tia." *MGG* V (1956), 55–57.

——— *22* (1936), 317 ff.
——— *26:*I (1954), ii.
Reaney *12* (1970), 40, 57.

20. GIAN TOSCANO; [75] Pit; 1 work, transcribed.

A

    Marrocco *6*:X.
    Pirrotta *26*:V; no. 47.

B

    Pirrotta *26*:V (1964), iii.
    Reaney *10* (1960), 39.

21. GIOVANNI DA CASCIA (JOHANNES DE FLORENTIA), *fl.* 1350; 1; Florence, then Verona, also Visconti and della Scala courts; *Sq*, *FP*, Lo, Pit, PR, Rs, Grot; 19 works, all transcribed.

A

    * Marrocco *6:VI*, 21–78; 19 works.   ParrishT, 79.
    * Pirrotta *26*:I; nos. 2–20, 39.   Riemann *2*, I:2, 309.
    WolfSq, 3–14; 12 works.   RiemannMB; no. 3.
    CorteSc; no. 24.   ScheringGB; no. 22.
    Einstein. *A Short History of Music.*   Schering *5*, 70.
       2d American ed., rev. and enl.   Wolf *4*, 633.
       New York, Knopf, 1938, 265.   ——— *5*:III; nos. 38, 39.
    Ellinwood *1*, 55.   ——— *6*:I, 297, 305.
    ——— *3*, 33.   ——— *10*:II, 69.
    Marrocco *3;* nos. 4, 15, 29.

B

    Apel *3* (1953), 386.
    Carducci *2* (1929), 366–367.
    Casimiri (1934).
    Ellinwood *1* (1960), 74.
    Ghisi *3* (1962), 51.
    Günther *7* (1962–63), 15.
    Haas (1931), 98–99.
    Königslöw (1940), 12–13.
    LiGotti. "Il più antico polifonista del secolo XIV, Giovanni da Cascia."
       Italica XXIV (1947), 196–200.
    LiGotti *5* (1944), 49–50.
    Ludwig *1* (1904–05), 633.
    Marrocco *6*:VI (1967), ix.
    # Morini, A. "Un celebre musico dimenticato, Giovanni da Cascia." *Bolletino*
       della regia . . . (Perugia, 1926), 305 ff.

---

75. Perhaps Johannes Florentinus? (Fischer *32*, 70 n. 344.)

Parrish *1* (1958), 76–78.
 Analysis of "Con brachi assai."
Pirrotta. "Johannes de Florentia." *MGG* VII (1958), 90–92.
———— *26:*I (1954), i.
———— *36* (1935), 43–44.
Reaney *12* (1970), 56.
———— *14* (1966), 718.
 Suggestions for the performance of "O tu, cara scientia."
Villani, 34.
WolfSq (1955), Introduction, ix.
Wouters (1954), 62–63, 124, 126.

22. GIOVANNI DA FOLIGNO (JOHANNES FULGINATE [?]); Luc; 1 work, transcribed.

A

Marrocco *6:*X.

B

Pirrotta *10:1* (1949), 137.

23. GRAZIOSO (GRATIOSUS) DA PADOVA; PadA; 1 work, transcribed.

A

Marrocco *6:*X.

B

Ellinwood *1* (1960), 80.

24. GUGLIELMO DI FRANCIA [76] (GUILELMUS PARIGINUS; FRATE GUGLIELMO DI SANTO SPIRITO; GUILELMUS MONACHUS); II; Florence; Lo [Sq, Pit?]; 3 [+3?] works, transcribed.

A

Marrocco *6:*IX; 3 works.

* Pirrotta *26:*V; nos. 31–36:6.
———— *36;* no. 7 (analyzed, p. 73).

B

See **EGIDIO.**

---

76. See **EGIDIO** for remarks on both men, also for works with both names appearing.

HENRICUS, see ARRIGO.

JACOBELUS BIANCHY, see BIANCHY.

25. JACOPO DA BOLOGNA (JACOBUS DE BONONIA), d. *ca.* 1360; I; active
    in northeastern Italy, court of Verona; *Sq*, FP, PR (here anonymous), Pit,
    Lo, Grot; 33 [+2?] works, all [?] transcribed.[77]

    A

    * Marrocco *6:*VI, 80–168; 33 works.   *HistS,* 19.
    * ———— 7.   Hus; no. 20.
    * Pirrotta *26:*IV; nos. 1–33.   Marrocco *3;* nos. 12, 21, 26.
    WolfSq, 17–44; 27 works.   Osthoff, suppl.; no. 1.
    Bartha, 23.   ReeM, 363.
    Besseler *11,* 158.   Riemann *2,* I:2, 315.
    Fischer 7, 266, 269.   Torchi; no. 1.
    GleE, 99.   Wolf *5:III;* nos. 40–42.
    HAM; no. 49.   ———— *6:*I, 321.
    Harman, 159.

    B

    Apel *3* (1953), 374–376.
    Carducci *2* (1929), 366–367.
    Ellinwood *1* (1960), 75–76.
    Fischer *6* (1962), 19, 22–23.
    ———— 7 (1958–61).
       Author, by means of stylistic analysis of these unica in PR, suspects that
       they are by Jacopo, though they were previously thought to be anony-
       mous.
    ———— *15* (1957), 41.
    Ghisi *12* (1959).
       By means of a polyphonic lauda of Jacopo, the evolution of Italian
       polyphony in the fourteenth and fifteenth centuries is demonstrated.
       The lauda, when rewritten without the vocal melismas, approaches the
       fifteenth-century style.
    HistS (1953), 21.
    Königslöw (1940), 13–15.
    LiGotti *5* (1944), 51–54.
    Ludwig *1* (1904–05), 634.
    ———— *3* (1930), 282–283.
    Marrocco *6:*VI (1967), ix.
    ———— 7 (1954), Preface.
    Pirrotta. "Jacobus de Bononia." *MGG* VI (1957), 1619–1625.

    ---
    77. See Fischer 7, Section B.

———— *26*:IV (1963), i–ii.
———— *36* (1935), 43–44.
Plamenac *2* (1955), 174.
———— *4* (1964), 146.
    Regarding "Prima virtut . . ." and "Vestisse la cornachia."
Reaney *12* (1970), 56.
Riemann *4* (1905–06), 536.
Ward, John. "W. Thomas Marrocco's *The Music of Jacopo Bologna.*"
    JAMS VIII (1955), 36–41.
    A scholarly and well-documented review of the Marrocco publication,
    which discusses the music in detail and contributes to the knowledge of
    Jacopo.

26. JACOPO PIANEL(L)AIO (DA FIRENZE); II [?]; Lo; 1 work, transcribed.

    A

    Marrocco *6*:X.
    Pirrotta *26*:V; no. 46.

    B

    Pirrotta *26*:V (1964), iii.
    "No biographical information; a name only."

27. JOHANNES BAÇUS CORREÇARIUS; PadA; 1 work, transcribed.

    A

    Marrocco *6*:X.

28. JOHANNES FLORENTINUS (JOHANNES HORGANISTA DE FLOR-
    ENTIA; GIOVANNI MAZZUOLI "DEGLI ORGANI"), d. 1426; Str, Sq,
    Roquefort; 1 work, transcribed.

    The most illuminating remarks on this enigmatic figure have been made
    by Frank D'Accone (see section B below), who assumes that since a section
    was reserved for him in Sq, he must have been of considerable importance.
    For this reason he doubts that the inferior ballata, "Se tu di male . . . ,"
    from Pit is worthy of Mazzuoli, though Fischer suggests such a possibility,
    even while attributing it to Gian Toscano (see section B under GIAN
    TOSCANO). In considering the madrigal, "Quando amor gli occhi . . . ,"
    he again links the two figures, though this time favoring Johannes Flo-
    rentinus (Mazzuoli).

    A

    Fét *3*, 308.
    Pirrotta *26*:V; no. 49 (Appendix).

B

D'Accone. "Giovanni Mazzuoli; A Late Representative of the Italian Ars Nova." *Cert* II (1968), 23–38.
Elinwood *1* (1960), 75.
Fétis *3* (1876), 311 (from Roq).
Fischer *32* (1956), 34 n. 144, 70 n. 344.
Reaney *10* (1960), 39.
Wolf *5:*I (1904), 251.

29. LANDINI (LANDINO), FRANCESCO (FRANCESCO DEGLI ORGANI; IL CIECO; FRANCISCUS CAECUS), *ca.* 1325–1397; II; Florence; *Sq, FP,* Pit, Lo, PR, Luc, Sev, Str; [78] 155 [?] works, all transcribed.[79]

A

   * Ellinwood *4.*
   * Schrade *2.*
     With separate commentary.
   WolfSq, 197–316; 145 works.
   Bartha, 24a.
   CorteSc; no. 25.
   Ellinwood *1,* 66.
   ——— *2,* 206–216; 7 works.
   Fétis *3,* 312.
   GleE, 103, 104, 106, 108, 113; 5 works.
   Harman, 168.
   HistS, 21.
   Hus; nos. 17–19.
   Kiesewetter, Raphael G. *Geschichte der europäischabendländischen oder unserer heutigen Musik.* Supplement 3. Leipzig, Breitkopf & Härtel, 1846; no. 4.
   Ludwig *3,* 287.
   ———. "Musik des Mittelalters in der badischen Kunsthalle Karlsruhe." *ZfMW* V (1922–23), 459.
   Marrocco *3;* nos. 7, 10.
   OH I, 261.
   OH II, 321.
   ParrishM, 41 (analyzed, 40).
   Pirrotta *36;* nos. 9, 11, 12 (analyzed, p. 74).
   ReeM, 368.
   Riemann *2,* I:2, 330.
   ——— *2,* II:1, 86.
   RiemannHaus; no. 2.

---

78. Also scattered throughout other minor sources.
79. See Günther *1* regarding the possibility of two additional works of Landini in Pit, until recently thought to be anonymous.

RiemannMB; no. 5.
ScheringGB; no. 23.
Wolf *4*, 641.
—— *5*:III; nos. 51–53.
WolfME, 14.
Wolf *10*:I, 108.
—— *10*:II, 74, 216–218; four works.
WolfSS; no. 6.

B

Becherini *1* (1962), 170–178.
—— *2* (1962).
    References to Landini and to the role he played in the Italian Ars Nova are diffused throughout the article.
Besseler *11* (1931), 160–163.
Bonaccorsi *2* (1948), 594–595.
Borren *1* (1936).
    Concerning two of Landini's ballate that serve as bases for the polyphonic lauda.
—— *14* (1924), 65–66, 116.
Carducci. "Francesco Landini e i suoi contemporanei." *CorteA* (1945), 51–57.
    Some intimate details of early life not found elsewhere.
—— *2* (1929), 311–317.
Corsi *2* (1959), 331.
Einstein *1* (1949), 14–15.
Ellinwood *1* (1960), 77–80.
—— *2* (1936).
    An invaluable study of this composer. Work is divided according to type and chronology. The tritextual works and the composer's various devices are discussed. Seven compositions transcribed.
—— *4* (1939), Introduction.
    A discussion of early polyphony, Landini's contribution, the manuscript sources, notation, musical forms and style, the role of instruments, and methods of transcription.
EM II (1963), 565.
    A noteworthy article titled "F. Landini," and unsigned.[80]
Fétis *2* (1827), 107–108.
* Fischer *6* (1962), 25–31.
    Presents several points of view which might prove useful in arriving at a stylistic analysis of the works of Landini. The compositions are divided into three (and a possible fourth) types, each of which is determined by the specific functions of the three voices. These are clearly demonstrated by means of musical examples.

---

80. Prof. von Fischer informs me that he has written the article on Landini for a new edition of the *Enciclopedia della Musica* to be published by Rizzoli.

———— *12* (1957), 45–47.
———— *16* (1970), 17–28.
———— *17* (1964), 83, 84.
    Berlin fragment suggests Landini or Andreas; Ivrea fragment shows
the influence of Landini.
———— *34* (1966).
    In attempting to better establish chronology of works, the question is
approached through (1) problem of birthdate; (2) chronology as related
to manuscripts, forms, texts (including polytexts), notation, and iso-
rhythms; (3) texts as related to events; (4) style; and (5) grouping of the
works, which fall into three categories.
Gallo *1* (1968), 64.
    Regarding a ballata, also parts to another work, found in Sev.
Gandolfi. "Di una ballata con musica del secolo XIV." *NM* I:1 (Dec. 1896),
1–3.
————. "Una riparazione a proposito di F. Landino." *Rassegna nazionale*
X (1888), 58–71.
Ghisi *3* (1962), 51, 54–55.
Göllner. "Landini's 'Questa fanciulla' bei Oswald von Wolkenstein." *MF*
XVII (1964), 393–398.
    Regarding Landini's influence abroad in the first or second third of the
fifteenth century.
Haas (1931), 96–97.
Johnson, Martha. "A Study of Conflicting Key-Signatures in Francesco
Landini's Music." *Hamline Studies in Musicology* II. Hamline University,
1947, 27–39.
Königslöw (1940), 29–32.
LiGotti *5* (1944), 74–84.
———— "Una pretesa incoronazione di Francesco Landini." LiGotti *8* (1947),
91–97.
Ludwig *3* (1930), 279–281, 285.
Nolthenius. "Een autobiografisch Madrigal van F. Landini." *Tijdschrift
voor Muziekwetenschap* XVII (1955), 237–241.
    Regarding "Mostrammi amor," and in particular, "Fortuna gli tenea
la vista chiusa." ("Un pelegrin falcon"), no doubt related to his own
blindness.
Pirrotta. "Landini (Landino), Francesco." *MGG* VIII (1960), 163–168.
Plamenac *2* (1955), 172–174.
Reaney *12* (1970), 57–59.
ReeM (1940), 362–368, 372–373.
Schachter, Carl. "Landini's Treatment of Consonance and Dissonance: A
Study in 14th Century Counterpoint." *Music Forum* II (1970), 130–186.
    An original and unorthodox approach to fourteenth-century harmony.
Schneider *2* (1963).
    Dealing with his use of the free melisma and its connection with
Mediterranean music making and the Indo-European custom.
Schrade *2* (1958), Commentary.
    Discusses some disadvantages of Ellinwood *4,* and states his reasons

for a new edition of Landini's works. Painstaking and detailed comments on Trecento music, with reference to sources, forms, literary texts, rhythmic characteristics. Commentary on each composition is divided into sources, literary texts, rhythm, special notes, and editions. Bibliography.

Seay 2 (1965), 160–164.

Villani, 34.

Wesselofsky I, 23, 24, 43, 100–109; III, Appendix X, 3–5, 112–113.

Wolf 4 (1901–02), 613–616.

WolfSq (1955). Introduction, ix–xii.

Wouters (1954), 64–78, 127–129.

This author, as Schachter (see above), discusses the "Landini cadence." Although the term is used frequently, Parrish (ParrishM, 40) points out that this device is not peculiar to Landini, since it is employed by most Trecento composers. Musical examples.

30. LANTINS (LANCTIUS, LANTINIS, LANTIUS, LATINIS), HUG(H)O (UGO) DE, 1st half of fifteenth century; perhaps from Liège; Venice; Bari [?]; [81] used mainly French texts; O; 2 [+2?] works, transcribed.

A

Borren P; nos. 29–32.[82]

Marrocco 6:X; 2 works.

B

Borren 8 (1960), 235–236.

———. "Hugo et Arnold de Lantins." *Fédération archaéologique et historique de Belgique* XXIX (Congrès de Liège, 1932), 263–272.

Pirrotta 30 (1966), 675–676.

Reaney 6 (1970), 450, 451.

Rehm, Wolfgang. "Lantins (Lantinis, Latinis, Lantius, Lanetius), Hugo (Hugho, Ugo) de." *MGG* VIII (1960), 200–202.

31. LORENZO (MASINI) DA FIRENZE (LAURENTIUS MASII), fourteenth century; II; Florence; *Sq*, Lo, FP, Pit, Rs; 16 [+1?] works, 16 transcribed.

A

* Marrocco 6:VIII, 120–171; 16 works.
* Pirrotta 26:III; nos. 2–17.
* WolfSq, 77–96; 16 works.

Bonaventura 1, 422, 427.

Hus; no. 21.

Main, 148.

Marrocco 3; no. 1.

Pirrotta 36; no. 1 (analyzed, p. 71).

Wolf 5:III; no. 49.

——— 10:II, 70, 213.

——— 12, 65.

---

81. Is known to have written at least one motet dedicated to a doge of Venice. Perhaps was a papal singer at Bari (*MGG* VIII, 200).

82. Texts partially Latinized. Two are ballata refrains.

B

Bonaventura *1* (1914), 416–419.
Regarding two ballate with texts by Boccaccio.
Königslöw (1940), 17–19.
Ludwig *1* (1904–05), 635.
Main (1965).
An analysis of "A poste messe," which takes exception to all transcriptions heretofore, and presents this new one as "the first correct transcription to appear in print."
Marrocco 5 (1970), 419.
Regarding his mastery of integrated devices.
———— 6:VII (1971), Introduction.
Pirrotta. "Laurentius de Florentia." *MGG* VIII (1960), 419.
———— 22 (1936), 317 ff.
————26:III (1962), i–ii.
Villani, 34.

32. MATTEO (MELCHIOR) DA BRESCIA (MATHEUS DE BRIXIA; PREPOSITUS BRISIENSIS); Padua cathedral, 1411–1425; O; 4 works, transcribed.

A

Marrocco 6:X; 4 works.

B

Fano *3* (1956), 14.
Gallo. *Ricerche sulle origini della cappella musicale del Duomo di Vicenza.* Vicenza, 1964, 23–27.
Reaney 6 (1970), 455.
Wolf 2 (1899–1900), 154.

33. MATTEO DA PERUGIA (MATHEUS DE PERUSIO), d. *ca.* 1418; Milan; wrote chiefly sacred compositions, and mainly in the French style ("22 out of 30 are French songs"); [83] Mod; 2 works, transcribed.

A

Fano *3*, 323, 328 (analyzed, 441–449).

Marrocco 6:X; 2 works.

B

Apel *1* (1950), 2, 4, 8, 9, 10, 13–14, 19, 20, 21.
Besseler. "Hat Matheus de Perusio Epoche gemacht?" *MF* VIII (1955), 19–23.

---

83. Reaney *1*, 302.

Challenges Apel's position (Apel *1*, 13–14) regarding the role of Matteo. Feels that Apel's theory that the "modern style" was created by Matteo is not tenable and does not consider Matteo a "key figure."

Fano *2* (1953).

———— *3* (1956), 14–23, 41–70.

Special reference to the two Italian pieces, p. 56.

Fischer *9* (1959).

Gombosi (1950), 603–607.

Günther *8* (1964), 184.

Korte *2* (1933), 13, 14.

Pirrotta *11* (1946), 46–58.

Reaney. "Matteo da Perugia (Matheus de Perusio)." *MGG* VIII (1960), 1793–1794.

———— *12* (1970), 62.

ReeR (1959), 31.

Sartori *1* (1956), 12–23.

Wouters (1954), 142.

MAZZUOLI, see JOHANNES FLORENTINUS

34. NIC(C)OLO DA PERUGIA (DEL PROPOSTO; NICOLAUS PRAEPOSITUS), fourteenth century; II; Tuscany; *Sq*, Lo, Pit, Luc; 41 works, all transcribed.

A

* Marrocco *6*:VIII, 101–198; 41 works.

WolfSq, 119–156; 36 works.[84]

Disertori, xiii.[85]

Marrocco *3;* nos. 9, 14, 19, 24.

Pirrotta *10:II,* 150.

———— *36;* nos. 2–6, 8, 10 (analyzed, pp. 72–74).

Schering *5*, 74.

Wolf *5:*III; nos. 54–55.

WolfME, 16.

WolfSS; no. 7.

---

84. Fischer (*32*, 41) has ascribed p. 141 to Paolo.
85. In the "new style, heralding the frottola" (Disertori).

B

Ellinwood *1* (1960), 77.
Fischer. "Nicolaus de Perugia."
  MGG IX (1961), 1456–1457.
Ghisi *3* (1962), 51–52, 53.
Königslöw (1940), 20, 22.
LiGotti *5* (1944), 73–74.
Ludwig *1* (1904–05), 636.
Marrocco *6*:VIII (1972[?]), Intro-
  duction.

Pirrotta *10:II* (1950), 148–149.
——— *10:III* (1951), 122.
——— *22* (1936), 320.
——— *36* (1935), 47.
Reaney *12* (1970), 40.
  Regarding a monodic ballata.
ReeM (1940), 362.
Wouters (1954), 64.

35. NUCELLA; III; Str; 1 work, transcribed.[86]

A

Marrocco *6*:X.

B

Borren *2* (1924), 528–529.

36. PAOLO (TENORISTA) DA FIRENZE (DOMINUS PAULUS; DOMPNI
PAULI; DON PAGHOLLO), b. 1355–1360; III; member of Capponi family;
Camoldolite monk; theorist also; place reserved for him in Sq; worked in
north, though works appear in manuscripts of Florentine tradition; *Pit,*
NYL, Lo; 33 [+4?] works, 33 transcribed.[87]

A

* Marrocco *6*:IX; 33 works.[88]
Günther *9*, 115.
Monterosso, Raffaello. "Un 'auctoritas' dantesca in un madrigale dell' Ars
  Nova." *CHM* IV (1966), 188.
Pirrotta *33*, 69–81; 5 works.[89]
RiemannHaus; no. 1.
Wolf *4*, 644.
——— *5*:III; no. 61.
——— *10*:II, 76, 219.

86. Forthcoming. This ballata, "De bon parole," is a unicum and almost illegible. It
has therefore presented transcription problems.
87. Should further studies confirm Günther's suspicion that some twelve compositions
in Pit, until now thought to be anonymous, are by Paolo, these figures would obviously be substantially altered. See Günther *1*.
88. Perhaps *not* a complete edition? See n. 87.
89. Pirrotta assumes (?) p. 72 to be by Paolo, since the style is closely related, and
calls this a "valuable addition to the Ars Nova repertory."

B

Apel *3* (1953), 394, 398, 407–408.
Becherini *1* (1962), 159–169.
Ellinwood *1* (1960), 77.
Fischer *16* (1970), 19–28.
——— *22* (1969).
———. "Paulus de Florentia." *MGG* X (1962), 965–968.
——— *33* (1958), 187.
Ghisi *3* (1962), 52.
Günther *1* (1966).
> Recent treatment with infrared rays has made possible a comparison of hands and signatures found in Pit. As a result, this author is inclined to attribute some twelve compositions heretofore thought anonymous to Paolo.

——— *9* (1967).
> Regarding the date of "Godi . . ." and regarding Pit.

Harrison (1966), 334–335.
> Regarding "Godi . . ." and the possible use of the pipe and tabor in its performance.

Königslöw (1940), 32–34.
LiGotti, and N. Pirrotta. "Paolo Tenorista, fiorentino extra moenia," *Estudios dedicados a Menendez Pidal* III (Madrid, 1952), 577–606.
Marrocco. "Paolo Tenorista in a new Fragment of the Italiana Ars Nova." *JAMS* XV:2 (summer 1962), 213–214.
> A review of Pirrotta *33*.

Monterosso *1* (1966).
> Regarding his madrigal, "Godi, Firenze." Was the text composed by Dante or by Paolo himself? Points out Paolo's liking for humanistic poets, particularly Dante.

Pirrotta *10:II* (1950), 125 n. 13.
——— *10:III* (1951), 141–142.
———. "Paolo da Firenze in un nuovo frammento dell'Ars Nova." *MD* X (1956), 61–66.
——— *33* (1961), 17–56.
> A study of Paolo and of the five compositions contained in the fragment. Documentary footnotes and inventory of Paolo's works. Notice is taken of the striking similarity between the coat of arms appearing in Pit and the heraldic device employed by the Capponi.

——— *36* (1935), 45, 47. (I)
Reaney *10* (1960), 34–35.
Seay *3* (1962).
> Regarding his role as a theorist. More on this in Section VII (Trecento Theory).

Termini, Francesco. "Don Paolo." Unpublished doctoral dissertation. University of Southern California, 1956.

37. PAOLO ROSSO (PETRUS RUBEUS?); O; 2 works, transcribed.

A

Clercx 7, 167.
Marrocco 6:X; 2 works.

B

Clercx 4:I (1960), 69.
———— 8 (1961), 161, 166.
Reaney 6 (1970), 455.

PETRUS RUBEUS, see PAOLO ROSSO

PIANEL(L)AIO, see JACOPO PIANEL(L)AIO

38. PIERO, MAGISTER, fourteenth century; I, active in northern Italy, enter-
ing competitions in Milan and Verona; *FP*, Rs; 8 [+2?] works, 8 transcribed.

A

* Marrocco 6:VI; 2-20; 8 works.   OH I, 265.
* Pirrotta 26:II; nos. 1-8.   Toguchi 2, 75.
Marrocco 3; nos. 3, 5, 6, 17,   Wolf 4, 639.
   23 a/b [90]: 5 works.   ———— 5:III; no. 56.
HistS, 23.   ———— 10:II, 75.

B

Becherini 4 (1964), 24-25.
    Concerning the caccia, "Con brachi assai. . . ."
Ellinwood 1 (1960), 76.
Fischer. "Piero." *MGG* X (1962), 1261-1263.
HistS (1933), 24.
Königslöw (1940), 11-12.
LiGotti 5 (1944), 50-51.
Ludwig 1 (1904/05), 634.
———— 3 (1930), 282-285.
Marrocco 6:VI (1967), ix.
    To the effect that his name appears only in FP, though there are two
    works in Rs.
Pirrotta 26:II (1960), i, ii.
———— 35 (1962).
    Contrary to his views expressed earlier,[91] the author now feels that the

---

90. Previously published as anonymous.
91. Pirrotta 34:I, 305-323.

development of the caccia was rapid, and that Piero, more than any other single composer, contributed to this development.

Riemann *4* (1905–06), 546.
Toguchi *2* (1970), 69–74.
Wouters (1954), 63–64, 126.

39. RANDOLFUS ROMANUS, late fourteenth century, early fifteenth century [?]; singer, Treviso cathedral, 1426; O; 1 work, transcribed.

A

Marrocco *6:*X.
Stainer, 181.

B

EitQ VIII, 127.
Reaney *6* (1970), 452, 455–456, 462.
———— *9* (1955), 78, 90.

REYNALDUS, see FRANCISCUS

40. ROSSO COLLEGRANO (DA C[H]OLLEGRANA), fourteenth century; Tuscany [?]; Lo; 1 work, transcribed.

A

Marrocco *6:*VII, 27.   Wolf *5:*III; no. 60.
Pirrotta *26:*III; no. 35.

B

Ludwig *1* (1904–05), 638.   Reaney 7 (1958), 71.[92]
Pirrotta *26:*III (1960), ii.   Wolf *5:*I (1904), 267.[93]

41. UGOLINO D'ORVIETO, *ca.* 1380–1457; Ferrara, *ca.* 1425–30; chiefly theory, but some music; Cas; 2 works, transcribed.

A

Marrocco *6:*X; 2 works.
Seay *5*, 164.

B

Haberl *1* (1895).
    With valuable documentary footnotes.
Kornmüller (1895).

---

92. Feels he may be the P. Rosso of O and BL Q15.
93. Cited only.

Seay 5 (1955).

Points out that Ugolino was a transitional figure between the Middle Ages and the Renaissance. Discusses the rhythmic complexities of his notation. For more on theory, see entries under Seay in Section VII (Trecento Theory).

42. VINCENZO D'ARIMINI (DA RIMINI; ABATE VINCENTIUS DA IMOLA), *ca.* 1330–1370; I; Florence and Bologna [?]; *Sq*, Lo, Pit; 6 works, all transcribed.

A

* Marrocco 6:*VII*, 1–21; 6 works.   Marrocco 3; nos. 13, 16.
* Pirrotta 26:IV; nos. 36–41.   Wolf 5:III; no. 50.
* WolfSq, 65–74; 6 works.

B

Ellinwood 1 (1960), 77.   Marrocco 3 (1961), xviii.
Königslöw (1940), 15.   ———— 6:VII (1971), Introduction.
LiGotti 5 (1944), 70.   Pirrotta 26:IV (1963), ii–iii.
Ludwig 1 (1904–05), 636.

43. ZACHARA (ZACHERA) DA TERAMO (A. ZACARA; ANTHONIUS CLERICUS [?],[94] early fifteenth century; III; northern Italy [?]; *Luc* (Perugia fragment), O, Pz (as anonymous); 9 [+1] works, all transcribed.

A

* Marrocco 6:X; 10 works.
Ghisi 11, 13–15; 3 works.[95]
Pirrotta 10:II, 151 (discussion of,
    p. 149).
Plamenac 6, 318/319.[96]

B

Bonaccorsi 2 (1948), 588–590.
Borren 2 (1924), 529–531.

On the perplexing problem posed by the given name Anthonius and its diminutive Anthonellus, with a recommendation for comparative analysis of works as a possible means of clarification.

Fisher 12 (1957), 47.
———— 32 (1956), 51 n. 238.

---

94. Marrocco ascribes the ballata, "E, ardo in un fugo," found in Str to Zachara, no doubt having followed the procedure recommended by Borren (Borren 2). For this composition, see also Fischer 32, 51 n. 238.

95. Page 14 has mixed Latin and Italian text.

96. Without words, for keyboard instrument.

Linking Zacara with Anthonius.

────── *33* (1958), 188.

Ghisi *3* (1962), 53.

────── *8* (1942), 84–86, 91–92.

────── *14* (1962), 37.

Pirrotta *10:III* (1951), 136–137.

────── *11* (1946), 43 n. 1.

Reaney *1* (1960), 301.

────── *6* (1970), 455, 457.

────── *12* (1970), 61.

──────. "Zachara und Zacharias." *MGG* XIV (1968), 960–963.

Under the caption "Zachara u. Zacherias" it is conceded that there are "at least two musicians. . . ." The first, for years unknown, seems somewhat older than the second. There is some speculation regarding a third musician.

44. ZACHERIAS, MAGISTER NICOLA (ZACHARIA; ZACCARIA) CDNP (Cantor Domini Nostra Papae) [ZACHERIE?],[97] late fourteenth century, early fifteenth; early years in Milan; papal service, 1420; *Sq*, Mod, O, Luc; 7 [+1?] works, 7 transcribed.

A

* Marrocco *6*:X; 7 works.   Marrocco *3*; no. 2.
* WolfSq, 325–332; 7 works.   Wolf *4*, 618.
Ficker *2*, 152.   ────── *5*:III; no. 63.

B

Borren *9* (1941), 121.

Ghisi *8* (1942), 91, 92.[98]

────── *10* (1946), 185.

Königslöw (1940), 35.

Korte *2* (1933), 76.

LiGotti *5* (1944), 96.

Ludwig *1* (1904–05), 639.

Main (1965), 143 n. 41.

Pirrotta *10:III* (1951), 135–136.

────── *11* (1946), 41–43.

────── *36* (1935), 45 n.

Reaney *1* (1960), 301.

In agreement with Ludwig and Wolf, it is suspected that this composer and Zacherie, priest of the Brindisi diocese, may be one and the same.

────── *6* (1970), 457

---

97. Many of the references cited above deal with speculation regarding another composer with a similar name. See in particular Ghisi *5*, Pirrotta *10*:III, n. 66, Pirrotta *11*, n. 1. See also EitQ X, 317; Fischer *32*, 7, 8; Fischer *33*, 188.

98. Or see Ghisi *5*, 27–28 (German version of Ghisi *8*).

Points out that in O, Antonio Zacara is clearly distinguished from
Nicola Zacharie.

———— *17* (1968).

See above, under ZACHARA.

ReeM (1940), 373.

ReeR (1959), 31.

WolfSq (1955), Introduction, xii.

45. ZACHERIE, NICOLAUS, early fifteenth century [?]; priest of Brindisi
Diocese; O; 1 [?] work, transcribed.

A

Marrocco *6*:X.

B

Fischer *32* (1956), 7.

Korte *2* (1933), 75.

Pirrotta *10:III* (1951), 135.

———— *36* (1935), 45 n.
To the effect that *Zacharie,* being the genitive, could very well indicate
that he is the son of Magister Zacharias, CDNP.

WolfSq (1955), Introduction, xii.

46. ZANINO [ZAN(N)INUS] DE PERAGA DE PADUA, early fifteenth century
[?]; Dom; 1 work, transcribed.

A

Ghisi *11*, 21.

Marrocco *6*:X.

B

Ghisi *10* (1946), 183.[99]

LiGotti *5* (1944), 90.[100]

ANONYMOUS WORKS, BY CODEX (VIII b)

These works are grouped under manuscript sources. Section A lists the works
in transcription, following the same arrangement as that employed in VIII a
(see p. 75). Section B lists only that literature pertaining specifically to the
transcriptions indicated in section A. For complete information on the manuscripts cited here, see Manuscript Sources, V b and V c, above.

---

99. Cited only.
100. Cited only. See also Sabbadini.

1 work from BOLOGNA, CIVICO MUSEO BIBLIOGRAFICO MUSICALE, Q16 (olim Liceo musicale) [101]

A

Ghisi *5*, 38.

B

Ghisi *8* (1942), 98, 99–100.
Novati (1906–07), 317 n. 3.

5 works from BOLOGNA, BIBL. UNIVERSITARIA 2216 (BU).

A

Marrocco *6*:XI; nos. 37, 61, 68, 89.
Gallo *6;* no. 3.
Ghisi *11*, 17.

1 work from DOMODOSSOLA FRAGMENTS, CONVENTO DI MONTE CALVARIO, MS 14, now at Stresa, Collegio Rosmini (Dom).

A

Marrocco *6*:XI; no. 9.

1 work from ESCORIAL IV. α. 24 (Esc, EscB).

A

Marrocco *6*:XI; no. 53.

2 [?] works from FAENZA, BIBL. COMUNALE 117 (Bonadies, Fa).

A

Marrocco *6*:XI; no. 12.
Plamenac *4*, 157.

B

Plamenac *4* (1964), 145.
    Regarding a keyboard arrangement of "Deduto sey" from BU and Pz.

---

101. This codex is not a source of Italian Ars Nova music, but the caccia found here, dating from about the mid-fifteenth century, is cited by Ghisi as an example of the evolution of the caccia.

9 works from LONDON, BRITISH MUSEUM, Add 29987 (Lo).

A

Marrocco *6*:XI; nos. 13, 14, 21, 35,   *HAM;* no. 51.
   48, 59, 60.   Marrocco *3;* no. 23.[103]
Pirrotta *26*:III; nos. 39–44.[102]   ——— *6*:VIII, 77, 89.
Bartha, 24c.   Pirrotta *26:II;* nos. 41, 43.
Einstein *2,* 265.

B

Fischer *32* (1956), 56 n. 266.
Pirrotta *26*:II (1960), ii.
——— *26*:III (1962), v, vi.

13 works from LUCCA, ARCHIVIO DI STATO, MS. 184 (Luc, Mancini, Man, Mn).

A

Marrocco *6*:XI; nos. 11, 18, 28, 29, 42, 45, 54, 56, 62, 63, 70, 82, 83.
Disertori, xi.
Marrocco *6*:VIII, 70.

B

Becherini *5* (1959), 246.
Bonaccorsi *2* (1948), 602, 608.[104]
Disertori (1954), xi.
Ghisi *10* (1946), 178, 179, 181.
   Regarding the similarity between the ballata "Mercè o morte" and
   Binchois' "Deuil angoisseux."
Pirrotta *10:II* (1950), 143.
——— *10:III* (1951), 140.

1 work from MODENA, BIBL. ESTENSE, *α*.M. 5,24 (olim lat. 568) (Mod, Est).

A

Marrocco *6*:XI; no. 88.

---

102. Scholars have previously attributed no. 42 ("Io son' un pellegrin") to Giovanni da Cascia, and it so appears in Bartha and *HAM.*

103. Here attributed as possibly to Piero. Published a few months earlier by Pirrotta (*26*:II, no. 43) as anonymous.

104. Here attributed to Binchois.

1 work from NEW YORK, PRIVATE LIBRARY OF PROFESSOR EDWARD E. LOWINSKY, now at Chicago (NYL).[105]

A

Marrocco *6:*XI; no. 31.

1 work from PADUA, BIBL. UNIVERSITARIA, Ms. 1115 (PadB).

A

Marrocco *6:*XI; no. 80.

25 works from PARIS, BIBL. NATIONALE, fonds italien 568 (Pit).

A

Marrocco *6:*XI; nos. 1, 3, 6, 8, 10, 15, 23–25, 27, 36, 40, 44, 46, 52, 55, 67, 74–76, 79, 81, 88.
———— *6:*VIII, 32, 96.
Pirrotta *26:*V; no. 48.

B

Günther 1 (1966).
The theory advanced here that sixteen works previously considered anonymous can now be attributed to Landini, Feo (or Andreas), and Paolo would alter substantially the total number of anonymous works. But Marrocco does not proceed on this hypothesis.

26 works from PARIS, BIBL. NATIONALE, nouv. acq. franç. 6771 (Reina, PR, R).[106]

A

Marrocco *6:*XI; nos. 5, 16, 19, 26, 30, 32–34, 38, 39, 41, 49, 58, 65, 66, 71, 77, 85, 87.
———— *6:*VIII, 5, 35, 44, 49, 61, 65, 91; 7 works.
Pirrotta *26:*II; nos. 34–40, 42.[107]
———— 27, 109.
Wilkins *3*, 83.

---

105. Listed by Pirrotta (*33*, 56) as an anonymous work, attributed to Paolo ("Dolce mia donna"). Considered by Marrocco as anonymous.

106. If one were to accept the theory advanced by Fischer (*7*), there would be only twenty-three anonymous works in this codex.

107. Nos. 36 and 39 published by Fischer (*7*) and attributed to Jacopo; no. 37 to Bartolino.

B

Fischer *15* (1957), 41, 45.
———— *33* (1958), 180, 194.
Pirrotta *26*:II (1960), ii.
———— *27* (1968).
Wilkins *3* (1965).

4 works from PARIS, BIBL. NATIONALE, nouv. acq. franç. 4917 (Pz, P 49).

A

Marrocco *6*:XI; nos. 22, 51, 64, 72.

2 works from PERUGIA, BIBL. COMUNALE, ms. 3065 (PerBC) Fragment of
LUCCA CODEX.

A

Ghisi *5*, 37.[108]

B

Ghisi *8* (1942), 97, 99.

2 works from PISTOIA, ARCHIVIO CAPITOLARE DEL DUOMO (Pist)
Fragment of LUCCA CODEX.

A

Disertori, xi.
Ghisi *11*, 17.
Marrocco *6*:XI; nos. 78, 84.

B

Ghisi *10* (1946).

2 works from ROME, BIBL. VAT. URB. lat. 1419 (RU$_1$).

A

Marrocco *6*:VIII, 43.
———— *6*:XI; no. 73.
Pirrotta *26*:III; no. 38.

---

108. Also found in Montecassino 871 (a fifteenth-century manuscript, not a source of
Italian Ars Nova music).

1 work from ROME, BIBL. VAT. URB. lat. 1411 (RU$_2$).

A

   Marrocco *6*:XI; no. 20.

33 [?] works from ROME, BIBL. VAT., Rossi 215 (Rossi, Rs); including the
OSTIGLIA FRAGMENT (RsO).

A

   Marrocco 6:VIII, 1, 3, 8–18, 22–30, 37–41, 47, 53–60, 68, 72, 75, 79, 81, 85,
      94, 95, 99; 29 works.
   Pirrotta *26*:II; nos 9–33.
   Crocker, Richard. *History of Musical Style.* N.Y., McGraw-Hill, 1966, 131.
   Ellinwood *1*, 37.
   Hus, 42, 44.
   Marrocco *3;* no. 18.[109]
   ——— *6*:XI; nos. 7, 17, 50, 57, 69.
   ——— *8*, 88 (Ostiglia fragment).
   Wolf *12*, 65–68; 4 works.

B

   Marrocco *8* (1967).
      Ostiglia fragment.
   Mischiati (1966).
      Ostiglia fragment.
   Pirrotta *12* (1959), 95.
   ——— *26*:II (1960), i.
   Wolf *12* (1938), 61, 62.

3 works from SIENA, ARCHIVIO DI STATO, 2 fragments (SieA, SieB).

A

   Ghisi *11*, 19 (SieA).
   ——— *15*, 176 (SieB).
   Marrocco *6*:XI; no. 4 (SieA); nos. 2, 90 (SieB).

B

   Ghisi *10* (1946), 182.

1 work from TRENT, CASTELLO DEL BUON CONSIGLIO, 87 (Tr. 87,
Tr).[110]

---

109. Pirrotta suspects this may be by Piero (Pirrotta *26*:II, no. 28; Pirrotta *33*, 59).
110. This codex is not a source of Italian Ars Nova music, but since it contains
the anonymous ballata "Gentile alma benigna" it has been taken into account.

A

DTO XI (22), 115.
Marrocco 6:XI; no. 43.

B

DTO VII (14–15) (1900), 35.
DTO XI (22) (1904), 137.
Ghisi *16* (1953), 62.

PRINCIPAL MODERN SOURCES OF
ITALIAN ARS NOVA MUSIC

COMPLETE EDITIONS

Clercx, Suzanne. *Johannes Ciconia: Un musicien liégeois et son temps.* Vol. II.
Bruxelles, Palais des académies, 1960. (Italian songs.)

Ellinwood, Leonard, ed. *The Works of Francesco Landini.* Cambridge, Mass.,
Mediaeval Academy of America, 1939. (Reissued 1949 by Edwards Bros., Ann
Arbor, Mich.)

Marrocco, W. Thomas, ed. *Fourteenth-Century Italian Cacce.* 2d ed., rev. and
expanded, Cambridge, Mass., Mediaeval Academy of America, 1961.

———, ed. *The Music of Jacopo da Bologna.* Berkeley and Los Angeles, University of California Press, 1954. (University of California Publications in
Music, no. 5.)

Schrade, Leo, ed. *The Works of Francesco Landini.* Monaco, Editions de
l'Oiseau-Lyre, 1958. (PMF, Vol. 4.)

COLLECTIONS [111]

Ghisi, Federico, ed. "Italian Ars Nova Music. . . ." *JRB* I:4 (1946).

Marrocco, W. Thomas, ed. *Fourteenth-Century Italian Cacce. . . .*[112]
———, ed. *Italian Secular Music.* Monaco, Editions de l'Oiseau-Lyre, 1967–.
6 vols. (*PMF*, vols. 6–11.)
  VI (1967). Magister Piero, Giovanni da Firenze, Jacopo da Bologna.
  VII (1971). Vincenzo da Rimini, Rosso de Collegrana, Donato da Firenze,
  Gherardello da Firenze, Lorenzo da Firenze.

---

111. A number of these contain within them complete editions of the works of some
composers, as indicated in Section VIII a with an asterisk. Minor composers (those with
fewer than *four* works) are not considered. Similarly, in the case of complete editions of
anonymous works, only the *major* codices are considered here.
112. This is both a complete edition (of cacce) and a collection (of cacce, both
anonymous and by various composers).

VIII (1972). Anonymous madrigals and cacce from Rs and other sources; Niccolò da Perugia.

IX (forthcoming). Bartolino da Padova, Egidius de Francia, Guilielmus de Francia, Don Paolo Tenorista da Firenze.

X (forthcoming). Andrea da Firenze, Antonello da Caserta, Bartolomeo de Bononia, Jacobelus Bianchi, Bartolomeo Brollo, Johannes Ciconia, Bonaiuto Corsini, Domenicus de Feraria, Guillaume Dufay, Maestro Feo, Giovanni da Foligno, Hugo de Lantins, Grazioso da Padova, Matteo da Brescia, Matteo da Perugia, Nucella, Jacopo Pianellaio, Fr[anciscus] Reynaldus, Antonius Romanus, Paolo Rosso, Randulfus Romanus, Andrea Stefani, Gian Toscano, Ugolino d'Orvieto, Antonio Zacara da Teramo, M. Zacherias Cantor, N. Zacherie, Zanino da Peraga.

XI (forthcoming). Anonymous ballate from Pit, PR, Luc, Lo, Rs, and other sources.

Pirrotta, Nino, ed. *The Music of Fourteenth-Century Italy*. Rome, American Institute of Musicology, 1954–1963. 5 vols. (*CMM* VIII, vols. 1–5.)

I (1954). The Florentines: Bartholus, Gherardellus, Giovanni da Cascia.

II (1960). Piero; anonymous works from Rs; anonymous madrigals and cacce from other sources.

III (1962). The Florentines: Donato, Lorenzo, Rosso da Collegrano; anonymous works from Lo and other sources.

IV (1963). Jacopo da Bologna and Vincenzo da Rimini.

V (1964). Andreas de Florentia, Guilielmus de Francia, Bonaiutus Corsini, Andrea Stefani, Ser Feo, Jacopo Pianelaio, Gian Toscano.

Wolf, Johannes. "Florenz in der Musikgeschichte des. 14. Jahrhunderts." *SIMG* III (1901–02), 599–646.

————, ed. "Musica fiorentina nel secolo XIV." *NM*, Supplement II.

————Sq (1955). Bartolino, Egidio, Gherardello, Lorenzo, Vincenzo, Zacherias.[113]

---

113. Worthy of mention are the twenty-five odd transcriptions scattered throughout Wolf 5:III, which have been cited in the body of this bibliography.

Appendix I

Bibliography of Works
Used in this Study, with Abbreviations

᠅

Numbers following imprint indicate pages where these works are cited in the body of this study. Italicized numbers refer to pages where transcriptions are cited.

Acta
: *Acta Musicologica*. Leipzig, 1928–. (Title varies.)

AfMF
: *Archiv für Musikforschung*. Leipzig, 1936–1943.

AfMW
: *Archiv für Musikwissenschaft*. Leipzig, 1918–.

AM
: *Annales musicologiques: moyen-âge et renaissance*. Paris, 1953–.

Anglés
: Anglés, Higinio. "The Musical Notation and Rhythm of the Italian Laude." In *Essays in Musicology: A Birthday Offering to Willi Apel*, ed. by Hans Tischler. Bloomington, Indiana, Indiana University School of Music, 1968, 51–60.
  36

Apel *1*   Apel, Willi, ed. *French Secular Music of the Late Four-
                        teenth Century.* Cambridge, Mass., Mediaeval Academy
                        of America, 1950.

                                              [13], 77, 94

Apel *2*   ———. "Imitation in the Thirteenth and Fourteenth
                        Centuries." In *Essays in Honor of Archibald Davison.*
                        Cambridge, Mass., Harvard University, Department of
                        Music, 1957, 25–38.

                                              36

Apel *3*   ———. *The Notation of Polyphonic Music, 900–1600.* 5th
                        ed. Cambridge, Mass., Mediaeval Academy of America,
                        1953.

                                        57, 62, 69, 86, 88, 97

Baker   Baker, Theodore. *Biographical Dictionary of Musicians.* 5th
                        ed., completely revised by Nicholas Slonimsky. New York,
                        Schirmer, 1958.

BarthaA   Bartha, Denes, ed. *A Zenetörténet Antologiaja.* Budapest,
                        Magyar Korus, 1948.

                                        88, 90, 104

Becherini *1*   Becherini, Bianca. "Antonio Squarcialupi e il codice Me-
                        diceo Palatino 87." *Cert* I (1962), 140–180.

                                     46 n. 32, 50–51, 50 n. 36, 91

Becherini 2   ———. "L'Ars Nova italiana del Trecento: strumenti ed
                        espressione musicale." *Cert* I (1962), 40–56.

                                        [13], 51, 52, 67, 91, 97

Becherini *3*   ———. "Communications sur Antonio Squarcialupi et notes
                        au Cod. Palatino 87." *RIMS* (Köln, 1958), 65.

                                              51

Becherini *4* ———. "Le insegne viscontee e i testi poetici dell'Ars Nova." In *Liber Amicorum Charles Van den Borren,* ed. by Albert Van der Linden. Anvers, Imprimerie Anversois, 1964, 17–25.

[13], 46, 46 n. 32, 98

Becherini *5* ———. "Poesia e musica in Italia ai primi del XV secolo." *Wég,* 239–259.

[13], 104

Besseler *1* Besseler, Heinrich. "Ars Nova." *MGG* I, 702–729.

[13], 36, 47, 57

Besseler *2* ———. "Bologna Kodex BL." *MGG* II, 95–99.

59

Besseler *3* ———. "Bologna Kodex BU." *MGG* II, 99–101.

60

Besseler *4* ———. "Ciconia, Johannes." *MGG* II, 1423–1434.

81

Besseler *5* ———. "Dufay." *MGG* III, 889–912.

83, 83 n. 73

Besseler *6* ———. "Dufay in Rom." *AfMW* XV (1958), 1–19.

83

Besseler *7* ———, ed. *Guillelmi Dufay: Opera Omnia,* Vol. VI. Rome, American Institute of Musicology, 1964. (*CMM,* 1.)

83, 83

Besseler *8* ———. "Hat Matheus de Perusio Epoche gemacht?" *MF* VIII (1955), 19–23.

94–95

Besseler *9*   ———. "Johannes de Muris." *MGG* VII, 105–111.
                                     70

Besseler *10*   ———. "The Manuscript Bologna Biblioteca Universitaria
                          2216." *MD* VI (1952), 39–65.
                                     60

Besseler *11*   ———. *Die Musik des Mittelalters und der Renaissance.*
                          Potsdam, Akademische Verlagsgesellschaft, Athenaion,
                          1931. (Handbuch der Musikwissenschaft, I. Ed. by
                          E. Bücken.)
                                     14, 26 n. 14, 26 n. 16, 36, 39 n. 25, *88,* 91

Besseler *12*   ———. "Neue Dokumente zum Leben und Schaffen Dufays."
                          AfMW IX (1951), 159–176.
                                     83

Besseler *13:I*   ———. "Studien zur Musik des Mittelalters. Neue Quellen
                          des 14. und beginnenden 15. Jahrhunderts." *AfMW* VII
                          (1925), 167–252.
                                     14, 47, 57, 59, n. 46 and 48, 60, 62, 63, 64, 65

Besseler *13:II*   ———. "Studien zur Musik des Mittelalters. . . ." *AfMW*
                          VIII (1926), 137–258.
                                     14, 60, 64

Bonaccorsi *1*   Bonaccorsi, Alfredo. "A. Stefani, musicista dell'Ars Nova."
                          RaM XVIII (1948), 103–105.
                                     76

Bonaccorsi 2   ———. "Un nuovo codice dell'Ars Nova: Il Codice Luc-
                          chese." *Atti della accademia nazionale dei Lincei,* Ser. 8,
                          Vol. I:12 (1948), 539–615.
                                     15, 36, 54, 67, 76, 77, 77 n. 59, 78, 82, 91, 100, 104

Bonaventura *1*   Bonaventura, Arnaldo. "Il Boccaccio e la musica." *RMI* XXI
                          (1914), 405–442.
                                     15, 67, *93,* 94

Bonaventura 2 ————. *Dante e la musica.* Livorno, R. Giusti, 1904.
15, 18 n. 9, 67

Bonaventura 3 ————. "Musica e poesia del Trecento italiano." *Musica d'oggi* XVIII (1936), 3–7.
15

Borghezio Borghezio, G. "Un codice vaticano trecentesco di rime musicali." *Fédération archéologique et historique de Belgique* (Bruges, 1925), 231–232.
57

Borren 1 Borren, Charles Van den. "Actions et réactions de la polyphonie néerlandaise et la polyphonie italienne. . . ." *Revue belge d'archéologie et d'histoire de l'art* VI:1 (1936), 52 n. 1. (Reprinted in *RB* XXI (1967), 36–44.)
78, 91

Borren 2 ————. "L'apport italien dans un manuscrit du XVe siècle, perdu et partiellement retrouvé." *RMI* XXXI (1924), 527–533.
46, 66, 77, 96, 100, 100 n. 94

Borren 3 ————. "L'Ars Nova." *Wég*, 17–26.
15

Borren 4 ————. "The Codex Canonici 213 in the Bodleian Library at Oxford." *PRMA* LXXIII (1946), 45–58.
62

Borren 5 ————. "Le codex de Johannes Bonadies, musicien du XVe siècle." *Revue belge d'archéologie et d'histoire de l'art* X (1940), 251–261.
49, 67

Borren 6 ————. "Considérations générales sur la conjonction de la polyphonie italienne et de la polyphonie du Nord pendant la première moitié du XVᵉ siècle." *Institut historique belge de Rome,* Bull. XIX (1938), 175–187. (Reprinted in *RB* XXI (1967), 45–55.)

15, 62

Borren 7   ———. *Les débuts de la musique à Venise.* Bruxelles, Lombaerts, 1914.

45, 80

Borren *8*   ———. "Dufay and His School." *NOH,* 214–238.

67, 79, 83, 93

Borren *9*   ———. *Etudes sur le quinzième siècle musical.* Anvers, De Nederlandsche Boekhandel, 1941.

15, 47, 62, 66, 79, 83, 101

Borren *10*   ———. *Guillaume Dufay.* . . . Bruxelles, M. Hayez, 1925.

83

Borren *11*   ———. "Guillaume Dufay, centre du rayonnement de la polyphonie européenne à la fin du moyen âge." *Bulletin de l'institut historique belge* XX (1939), 171–185. (Reprinted in *RB* XXI (1967), 56–67.)

83

Borren *12*   ———. "Hugo et Arnold de Lantins." *Fédération archaéologique et historique de Belgique* XXIX (Congrès de Liège, 1932), 263–272. (Reprinted in *RB* XXI (1967), 29–35.)

93

Borren *13*   ———. "A Light of the Fifteenth Century: Guillaume Dufay." *MQ* XXI (1935), 279–297.

83

Borren *14*   ———. *Le manuscrit musical 222 C. 22 de la bibliothèque de Strasbourg.* . . . Anvers, E. Secelle, 1924. (Extrait des

> *Annales de l'académie royale d'archéologie de Belgique,* 1923.)
>
> 66, 91

BorrenP ———, ed. *Pièces polyphoniques profanes de provenance liégeoise (XVᵉ siècle)*. Bruxelles, Ed. de la Librairie Encyclopédiqie, 1950.

93

BorrenPS ———, ed. *Polyphonia sacra*. Nashdom Abbey, Burnham Bucks [and London], Plainsong and Mediaeval Music Society, 1932.

80

Bragard Bragard, Roger. "Le *Speculum musicae* du compilateur Jacques de Liège." *MD* VII (1953), 59–104; VIII (1954), 1–17.

70

Bridgman *1* Bridgman, Nanie. "Les illustrations musicales des oeuvres de Boccaccio dans les collections de la Bibliothèque nationale de Paris." *Cert* III (1970), 105–130.

15

Bridgman 2 ———. "Lauda." *Musica* I:3, 93–94.

36

Brown Brown, Howard. "Madrigale." *Musica* I:3, 227–229.

36

Buck Buck, August and B. Becherini. "Florenz," *MGG* IV, 367–394.

44

Bukofzer Bukofzer, Manfred. "Two Mensuration Canons," *MD* II (1948), 165–171.

54

Carapetyan *1*   Carapetyan, Armen, ed. *Anonimi. Notitia del valore delle note del canto misurato.* Rome, American Institute of Musicology, 1957 (*CSM*, 5).
15–16, 44, 70

Carapetyan 2   ————, ed. *An Early Fifteenth-Century Italian Source of Keyboard Music: The Codex Faenza, Biblioteca Comunale, 117.* A facsimile edition. (N.p.) American Institute of Musicology, 1961. (*Musicological Studies and Documents,* 10.)
49

Carapetyan *3*   ————. "A Fourteenth-Century Florentine Treatise in the Vernacular," *MD* IV:1 (1950), 81–92.
70

Carducci *1*   Carducci, Giosuè. "Francesco Landini e i suoi contemporanei," CorteA, 51–57.
91

Carducci 2   ————. "Musica e poesia nel mondo elegante italiano del secolo XIV." In his *Studi letterari.* Bologna, Zanichelli, 1929, 301–397. (For an earlier edition, see Appendix II.
16, 46, 84, 86, 88, 91

Casimiri   Casimiri, Rafaello. "Giovanni de Cascia e Donato da Cascia musicisti umbri?" *NA* XI (1934), 207–210.
82, 86

Cattin   Cattin, Giulio. *Contributi alla storia della lauda spirituale; sulla evoluzione musicale e letteraria della lauda nei secoli XIV e XV,* Bologna, 1958. (*Quadrivium, s.m.,* 2.)
36–37

Cellesi   Cellesi, Luigia. "Documenti per la storia musicale di Firenze." *RMI* XXXIV (1927), 579–602; XXXV (1928), 553–582.
44, 67

Cert

Certaldo. *L'Ars Nova italiana del Trecento*. Certaldo. Centro di studi sull'Ars Nova italiana del Trecento, 1962–1970. 3 vols.
I (1962) *Primo convegno internazionale, 23–26 luglio. 1959.*
II (1968) *Convegni di studio, 1961–1967.*
III (1970) *Secondo convegno internazionale, 17–22 luglio, 1969 sotto il patrocinio della Società internazionale di musicologia.*

Chambure

See Thibault

CHM

Collectanea Historiae Musicae, Florentiae, 1953–1966.

Cimbro

Cimbro, Attilio. "La musica e la parola dal trecento al cinquecento." *RaM* II (1929), 293–301.
16

Clercx *1*

Clercx, Suzanne. "Les accidents sous-entendus et la transcription en notation moderne." *Wég*, 167–195.
70

Clercx *2*

———. "Ciconia, Johannes." *EM* I, 480–481.
81

Clercx *3*

———. "Introduction" [Allocution prononcée au cours de la séance académique d'ouverture des Colloques de Wégimont II, 1955, l'Ars Nova]. *Wég*, 10–13.
16

Clercx *4*

———. *Johannes Ciconia: Un musicien liégeois et son temps.* Bruxelles, Palais des académies, 1960. 2 vols. Vol. I, Biography and criticism; Vol. II, Music.
16, 43, 46 n. 32, 47, 55, 59 n. 48, 60, 62, 63, 64, 70, *80*, 81, 98

Clercx *5*

———. "Johannes Ciconia de Leodio." *RIMS* (Utrecht, 1952), 107–126.
81

Clercx *6*   ————. "Johannes Ciconia et la chronologie des manuscrits italiens, Mod. 568 et Lucca (Mn)." *Wég*, 110–130.
47, 53 n. 41, 62, 81

Clercx 7   ————. "Propos sur l'Ars Nova." *RB* X (1956), 154–160.
16, 43, 45, 46, 48, 60, 63, 64, 78, 82, *98*

Clercx *8*   ————. "Le traité *De musica* de Georges Anselme de Parme." *RB* XV (1961), 161–167.
70, 98

CMM   *Corpus Mensurabilis Musicae.* Rome, American Institute of Musicology, 1947–.

Corsi *1*   Corsi, Giuseppe. "Frammenti di un codice musicale dell'Ars Nova rimasti sconosciuti." *Belfagor* XX:2 (1965), 210–215.
61

Corsi 2   ————. "Madrigali e ballate inediti del Trecento." *Belfagor* XIV (1959), 72–82, 329–341.
37, 82, 91

CorteA   Corte, Andrea, ed. *Antologia della storia della musica.* 4th ed. Torino, G. B. Paravia, 1945. (1937 edition has same contributors.)

Corte *1*   ————. *Le relazioni storiche della poesia e della musica italiana.* Torino, Pavia, 1936.
16–17

CorteSc   ————, ed. *Sceltà di musiche per lo studio della musica.* 2d ed. Milano, Ricordi, 1939.
85, 86, 90

Corte 2   ———— and G. Pannain. *Storia della musica.* Vol. I. Torino, 1944.
17

CouS   Coussemaker, Edmond de. *Scriptorum de Musica Medii Aevi, Novam Seriem.* . . . Paris, Durand, 1864–1876. 4 vols. Supersedes GerS.

Crocker   Crocker, Richard. *History of musical style.* New York, Mc-Graw-Hill, 1966.
              107

CSM   *Corpus Scriptorum de Musica* [Rome]. American Institute of Musicology, 1950–.

Culcasi   Culcasi, Carlo. *Il Petrarca e la musica.* Firenze, Bemporad, 1911.
              17

D'Accone *1* D'Accone, Frank. "Antonio Squarcialupi alla luce di documenti inediti." *Chigiana,* nuova ser. 3 (1966), 3–24.
              46, 51

D'Accone 2   ———. "Le compagnie dei laudesi in Firenze durante l'Ars Nova." *Cert* III (1970), 253–280.
              17

D'Accone *3* ———. "Giovanni Mazzuoli, a late Representative of the Italian Ars Nova." *Cert* II (1968), 23–38.
              90

Damerini *1* Damerini, Adelmo. "Introduzione al convegno . . . tenuto a Certaldo, . . . 1959." *Cert* I (1962), 3–17.
              17

Damerini 2   ———. "Lauda." *EM* II, 574–575.
              37

D'Ancona   D'Ancona, Paolo. *La miniatura fiorentina (sec. XI–XVI).* Firenze, Olschki, 1914.
              51

Dart   Dart, Thurston. *The Interpretation of Music.* 4th ed. London, Hutchinson, 1960, 147–172.
67

Davidsohn   Davidsohn, R. *Firenze ai tempi di Dante,* trans. by Eugenio D. Theseider. Firenze, R. Bemporad & Figlio, 1929.
17, 44

Debenedetti   Debenedetti, Santorre. "Un trattatello del secolo XIV sopra la poesia musicale." *Studi medievali* II (1906–1907), 59–82.
37, 41 n. 28

Disertori   Disertori, Benvenuto. *La frottola nella storia della musica.* Cremona, Athenaeum cremonense, 1954. (Extract from Instituta e monumenta, Ser. 1, I.)
53 n. 42, 77, 77, 95, *104*, 104

DTO   *Denkmäler der Tonkunst in Osterreich.* Wien, Universal, 1894–. Jahrgang VII (Vols. 14–15), *Sechs Trienter Codices . . . des XV Jahrhunderts,* ed. by G. Adler & O. Koller (1900). Jahrgang XI (vol. 22), *Sechs Trienter Codices . . . ,* ed. by G. Adler and O. Koller (1904).
108, 108

EC   *Encyclopédie de la musique et dictionnaire du conservatoire,* ed. by A. Lavignac & L. de la Laurencie. Paris, C. Delagrave, 1913–1931. 2 parts in 11 vol.

Eggebrecht   Eggebrecht, Hans Heinrich. "Der Begriff des 'Neuen' in der Musik von der Ars Nova bis zur Gegenwart." *RIMS* (New York, 1961:1), 195–202.
17

Einstein *1*   Einstein, Alfred. *The Italian Madrigal,* trans. by Oliver Strunk. Vol. I. Princeton, N.J., Princeton University Press, 1949.
17–18, 91

Einstein 2   ———. *A Short History of Music.* 2d American ed., rev. and
                        enl. New York, Knopf, 1938.
                                        86, 104

EitQ   Eitner, Robert. *Biographisch-bibliographisches Quellenlexi-
                        kon der Musiker und Musikgelehrten der Christlichen Zeit-
                        rechnung.* . . . Leipzig, Breitkopf & Härtel, 1900–1904.
                        10 vols.
                                        99, 101 n. 97

Ellinwood *1*   Ellinwood, Leonard. "The Fourteenth Century in Italy."
                        NOH, 31–80.
                        18, 37, 48, 51, 53, 55, 56, 57, 76, 78, 85, *86*, 86, 87, 88, 90, *90*,
                                        91, 96, 97, 98, 100, *107*

Ellinwood 2   ———. "Francesco Landini and His Music." *MQ* XXII
                        (1936), 190–216.
                                        18, *90*, 91

Ellinwood *3*   ———. "Origins of the Italian Ars Nova." *PAMS* (Dec.
                        1937), 29–37.
                                        18, 26 n. 14, *86*

Ellinwood *4*   ———, ed. *The Works of Francesco Landini.* Cambridge,
                        Mass., Mediaeval Academy of America, 1939. (Reissued
                        1949 by Edwards Bros., Ann Arbor, Mich.)
                                18, 37, 48, 51, 52, 53, 55, 56, 64, *90*, 91

EM   *Enciclopedia della musica.* Milano, Ricordi, 1963–64. 4 vols.
                                        91

Fano *1*   Fano, Fabio. "Ballata." *Musica* I:1, 316–318.
                                        37

Fano 2   ———. "Origini della cappella musicale del duomo di
                        Milano. Il primo maestro di cappella: Matteo da Perugia
                        (1402–16)." *RMI* LV (1953), 1–22.
                                        18, 45, 62, 95

Fano *3*   ————. *Le origini e il primo maestro di cappella: Matteo da Perugia.* Part I of *La cappella musicale del duomo di Milano.* Milano, Ricordi, 1956. (*IMAMI,* nuova ser., 1.)
                18, 45, 62, 67, 70, 77, 81, 94, *94,* 95

Fano *4*   ————. "Punti di vista su l'Ars Nova." *Cert* I (1962), 105–112.
                19, 81

Favaro   Favaro, Antonio. *Intorno alla vita e alle opere di Prosdocimus.* . . . Roma, 1879. (*Bolletino di bibliografia e di storia delle scienze matematiche e fisiche.* Jan.–Apr. 1879.)
                70

Fellerer   Fellerer, Gustav. "La 'Constitutio docta sanctorum patrum' di Giovanni XXII e la musica nuova del suo tempo." *Cert* I (1962), 9–17.
                19

Fétis *1*   Fétis, François. *Biographie universelle des musiciens.* . . . 1st ed. Paris, Firmin-Didot, 1835, Introduction, 195–199.
                55

Fétis 2   ————. "Découverte des manuscrits intéressans." *Revue musicale* I (1827), 107–113.
                55, 91

Fétis *3*   ————. *Histoire générale de la musique.* . . . Vol. V. Paris, Firmin-Didot, 1876.
                19, 89, 90, *90*

Ficker *1*   Ficker, Rudolf von. "Formprobleme der mittelalterlichen Musik." *ZfMW* VII (1924–25), 194–213.
                19, 26 n. 16, 60

Ficker 2   ————. "The Transition on the Continent." *NOH,* 134–164.
                19, 48, 62, 77, *101*

Fischer *1*   Fischer, Kurt von. "A propos de la répartition du texte et le
                    nombre de voix dans les oeuvres italiennes du Trecento."
                    Wég, 232–238.

                    67

Fischer *2*   ———. "Ars Nova." *EM* I, 123–124.

                    19

Fischer *3*   ———. "Una ballata trecentesca sconosciuta [e] aggiunte
                    per i frammenti di Siena." *Cert* II (1968), 39–47.

                    59, *85*, 85

Fischer *4*   ———. "Der Begriff des 'Neuen' in der Musik von der Ars
                    Nova bis zur Gegenwart." *RIMS* (New York, 1961:1), 184–
                    195.

                    19, 20 n. 11, 37

Fischer *5*   ———. "Chronologie des manuscrits du Trecento." *Wég*,
                    131–136.

                    48, 51, 52

Fischer *6*   ———. "Les compositions à trois voix chez les compositeurs
                    du Trecento." *Cert* I (1962), 18–31.

                    20, 37, 48, 88, 91

Fischer *7*   ———. "Drei unbekannte Werke von Jacopo da Bologna
                    und Bartolino da Padova?" *Miscelánea en homenaje a
                    monseñor Higinio Anglés* I (Barcelona, 1958–1961), 265–
                    281.

                    56, 56 n. 45, *78*, 78, *88*, 88, 105 nn. 106 and 107

Fischer *8*   ———. "Elementi arsnovistici nella musica boema antica."
                    Cert II (1968), 77–83.

                    20

Fischer *9*   ———. "G. Cesari–F. Fano: La Cappella musicale del
                    duomo di Milano. . . ." *MF* XII (1959), 223–230.

                    20, 95

Fischer *10*   ———. "Johannes Ciconia." *RB* XV (1961), 168–170.
                                        20

Fischer *11*   ———. "L'influence française sur la notation des manuscrits
                            du Trecento," *Wég*, 27–34.
                                        48, 70

Fischer *12*   ———. "Kontrafakturen und Parodien italienischen Werke
                            des Trecento und frühen Quattrocento." *AM* V (1957),
                            43–59.
                                        37, 66, 79, 81, 92, 100

Fischer *13*   ———. "Lucca, Codex." *MGG* VIII, 1249–1251.
                                        54

Fischer *14*   ———. "Il madrigale." *EM* III, 65.
                                        37

Fischer *15*   ———. "The manuscript Paris, Bibl. nat., nouv. acq. frç.
                            6771." *MD* XI (1957), 38–78.
                                        56, 78, 88, 106

Fischer *16*   ———. "Musica e società nel Trecento italiano." *Cert* III
                            (1970), 11–28.
                                        20, 46, 51, 92, 97

Fischer *17*   ———. "Neue Quellen zur Musik des 13., 14., und 15.
                            Jahrhunderts." *Acta* XXXVI (1964), 79–97.
                                        48, 59, 61, 92

Fischer *18*   ———. "Ein neues Trecentofragment." *Festschrift für
                            Walter Wiora*, ed. by L. Finscher and C. H. Mahling.
                            Basel and New York, Bärenreiter, 1967, 264–268.
                                        61

Fischer *19*   ———. "Nicolaus de Perugia." *MGG* IX, 1456–1457.
                                        96

Fischer *20*   ————. "On the Technique, Origin, and Evolution of
                        Italian Trecento Music." *MQ* XLVII:1 (Jan. 1961), 41–57.
                                    20, 26 n. 14, 37

Fischer *21*   ————. "Padua u. Paduaner Handschriften." *MGG* X, 571–
                        572.
                                    64

Fischer *22*   ————. *Paolo da Firenze und der Squarcialupi-Kodex.* Bo-
                        logna, 1969. (*Quadrivium, s.m.,* 9.)
                                    46, 51, 55 n. 43, 97

Fischer *23*   ————. "Paulus de Florentia." *MGG* X, 965–968.
                                    97

Fischer *24*   ————. "Piero." *MGG* X, 1261–1263.
                                    98

Fischer *25*   ————. "Quelques remarques sur les relations entre les
                        laudesi et les compositeurs florentins du Trecento." *Cert*
                        III (1970), 247–252.
                                    20, 46

Fischer *26*   ————. "Reina, Codex." *MGG* XI, 179–181.
                                    56

Fischer *27*   ————. "A Reply to N. E. Wilkins' Article on the Codex
                        Reina." *MD* XVII (1963), 75–77.
                                    56, 81

Fischer *28*   ————. "Die Rolle der Mehrstimmingkeit am Dome von
                        Siena zu Beginn des 13. Jahrhunderts." *AfMW* XVIII
                        (1961), 167–182.
                                    20

Fischer *29*   ————. "Squarcialupi, Antonio." *MGG* XII, 1096–1097.
                                    51

Fischer *30*   ———. "Squarcialupi Codex." *MGG* XII, 1097–1100.
                         51

Fischer *31*   ———. ". . . Der Squarcialupi-Codex." *MF* IX (1956), 77–
                         89.
                         51

Fischer *32*   ———. *Studien zur italienischen Musik des Trecento und*
                         frühen Quattrocento. Bern, Haupt, 1956. *(Publikationen*
                         der schweizerischen musikforschenden Gesellschaft. Ser. 2,
                         Vol. V.)
                         4, 20–21, 35 n. 24, 37, 46, 48, 51, 52, 52 n. 37, 53, 53 n. 42, 54,
                         55, 56, 57, 59 nn. 46 and 47, 62, 63 n. 52, 64, 65, 70, 77 nn. 59
                         and 60, 82, 84, 86 n. 75, 90, 95 n. 84, 100–101, 100 n. 94, 101
                         n. 97, 102, 104

Fischer *33*   ———. "Trecentomusik-Trecentoprobleme." *Acta* XXX
                         (1958), 179–199.
                         21, 43, 45, 48, 54, 56, 77 n. 59, 97, 101, 101 n. 97, 106

Fischer *34*   ———. "Ein Versuch zur Chronologie von Landinis
                         Werken." *MD* XX (1966), 31–46.
                         48, 92

Fischer *35*   ———. "[Zu Johannes Wolfs Ubertragung des] Squarcialupi-
                         Codex." *MF* IX (1956), 77–89.
                         51

Fischer *36*   ———. "Zur Ciconia-Forschung." *MF* XIV (1961), 316–322.
                         81

Fischer *37*   ———. "Zur Entwicklung der italienischen Trecento-Nota-
                         tion." *AfMW* XVI (1959), 87–99.
                         71

Frati *1*   Frati, Ludovico. "Frammento di un codice musicale del
                         secolo XIV." *Giornale storico della letteratura italiana*
                         XVIII (1891), 438–439.
                         64

Frati 2   ———. "Il Petrarca e la musica." *RMI* XXXI (1924), 59–68.
                                 21, 83

Gallo *1*   Gallo, F. Alberto. "Alcune fonti poco note di musica teorica
                                 e pratica." *Cert* II (1968), 49–76.
                                 65, 92

Gallo 2   ———, ed. Antonii Romani. *Opera.* Bologna, 1965. (*Anti-
                                 quae Musicae Italicae Monumenta Veneta.*)
                                 77

Gallo *3*   ———. "Antonius Romanus." *MGG,* suppl. I (1970?), 239–
                                 240.
                                 77

Gallo *4*   ———. *Il codice musicale 2216 della Biblioteca Universitaria
                                 di Bologna.* Bologna, 1968–70. 2 vols. Vol. I: Facsimile
                                 edition. Vol. II: Historical introduction, a new inventory,
                                 and transcriptions.
                                 60

Gallo 5   ———. *Mensurabilis Musicae Tractatuli.* Bologna, 1966. *An-
                                 tiquae Musicae Italicae Scriptores,* 1.)
                                 71

Gallo 6   ——— "Musiche veneziane nel ms. 2216 della Biblioteca
                                 Universitaria di Bologna." *Quadrivium* VI (1964), 107–111.
                                 With musical supplement.
                                 103

Gallo 7   ——— and Giovanni Mantese. *Ricerche sulle origini della
                                 cappella musicale del Duomo di Vicenza.* Venezia, Istituto
                                 per la collaborazione culturale, 1964.
                                 60, 94

Gallo *8*   ———. *La teoria della notazione in Italia della fine del
                                 XIII al inizio del XV secolo.* Bologna, Tamari, 1966. (*An-
                                 tiquae Musicae Italicae Subsidia Theorica,* 2.)
                                 71

Gallo *9*   ———. "La tradizione dei trattati musicali di Prosdocimo de Beldemandis." *Quadrivium* VI (1964), 57–82.

71

Gandolfi *1*   Gandolfi, Riccardo. "Di una ballata con musica del secolo XIV." *NM* I:1 (Dec. 1896), 1–3.

92

Gandolfi *2*   ———. *Illustrazioni d'alcuni cimeli concernenti l'arte musicale in Firenze.* Firenze, La Commissione per l'esposizione di Vienna, 1892. 28 pp. [29 leaves], 39 plates.

21, 51

Gandolfi *3*   ———. "Una riparazione a proposito di F. Landino." *Rassegna nazionale* X (1888), 58–71.

92

Gasperini   Gasperini, Guido. "L'art musical italien au XIVe siècle." *EC* I:2, 611–619.

21, 71

Gennrich   Gennrich, Friedrich. *Abriss der Mensuralnotation des XIV und der ersten Hälfte des XV Jahrhunderts.* Nieder-Modau, 1948. (*Musikwissenschaftliche Studienbibliothek,* 3–4.)

71

GerS   Gerbert, Martin. *Scriptores Ecclesiastici de Musica Sacra Potissimum.* . . . Silva Negra abbate, San-Blasianis, 1784. 3 vols. (Superseded by CouS.)

Ghisi *1*   Ghisi, Federico. "An Angel Concert in a Trecento Sienese Fresco." *ReeFest,* 308–313.

21, 67

Ghisi *2*   ———. "Angeli musicanti in una tavola attribuita al Giottino nel museo del Bargello di Firenze." *Cert* II (1968), 91–96.

22, 67

Ghisi *3* ————. "Gli aspetti musicali della lauda fra il XIV e il XV secolo, prima metà." In *Natalicia musicologica Knud Jeppesen,* ed. by Bjorn Hjelmborg and Søren Sørensen. Hafnia, W. Hansen, 1962, 51–57.
37–38, 76, 82, 84, 86, 92, 96, 97, 101

Ghisi *4* ————. "Bartolino da Padua." *MGG* I, 1349–1350.
78

Ghisi *5* ————. "Bruchstücke einer neuen Musikhandschrift der italienischen Ars Nova." *AfMW* VII (1942), 17–39.
54, 81, 101 nn. 97 and 98, *103, 106*

Ghisi *6* ————. "Caccia." *MGG* II, 604–609.
38

Ghisi *7* ————. "Danza e strumenti nella pittura senese del Trecento." *Cert* III (1970), 83–104.
22, 67

Ghisi *8* ————. "Frammenti di un nuovo codice musicale dell'Ars Nova italiana." *La Rinascità* V (1942), 72–103.
54, 81, 101, 101 n. 98, 103, 106

Ghisi *9* ————. "Un frammento musicale dell'Ars Nova italiana nell'Archivio capitolare della cattedrale di Pistoia." *RMI* XLII:2 (1938), 162–168.
54, 76

Ghisi *10* ————. "Italian Ars Nova Music: The Perugia and Pistoia Fragments of the Lucca Musical Codex and Other Unpublished Early Fifteenth-Century Sources." *JRB* I:3 (1946), 173–191.
46, 53 n. 41, 54, 60, 65, 77, 78, 81, 101, 102, 104, 106, 107

Ghisi *11* ————, ed. "Italian Ars Nova Music. . . ." *JRB* I:4 (1946). (Musical Supplement to Ghisi *10*)
53 n. 42, *100, 102, 103, 106, 107*

Ghisi *12*   ———. "La persistance du sentiment monodique et l'évolu-
                      tion de la polyphonie italienne du XIVᵉ au XVᵉ siècle."
                      Wég, 217–231.
                                    22, 26 n. 14, 38, 88

Ghisi *13*   ———. "Poesie musicali italiane. . . . " *NA* XV (1938), 36–
                      41, 189–196, 271–280.
                                    51, 52

Ghisi *14*   ———. "Rapporti armonici nella polifonia italiana del
                      Trecento." *Cert* I (1962), 32–39.
                                    22, 76, 84, 101

Ghisi *15*   ———. "A Second Sienese Fragment of the Italian Ars
                      Nova." *MD* II (1948), 173–177.
                                    65

Ghisi *16*   ———. "Strambotti e laude nel travestimento spirituale
                      della poesia musicale del Quattrocento." *CHM* I (1953),
                      45–78.
                                    38, 59 n. 48, 60, 76, 108

Ghislanzoni   Ghislanzoni, Alberto. "Les formes littéraires et musicales
                     italiennes au commencement du XIVᵉ siécle." *Wég*, 149–
                     163.
                                    38, 41 n. 28

GleE   Gleason, Harold, ed. *Examples of Music Before 1400*. Ro-
                     chester, N.Y., Eastman School of Music of the University
                     of Rochester, 1942.
                                    85, 88, 90

Göllner *1*   Göllner, Theodor. "Landini's 'Questa fanciulla' bei Oswald
                      von Wolkenstein." *MF* XVII (1964), 393–398.
                                    92

Göllner *2*   ———. "Die Trecento-Notation und der Tactus in der
                      ältesten deutschen Orgelquellen." *Cert* III (1970), 176–185.
                                    67, 71

Goldine

Goldine, Nicole. "Fra Bartolino da Padova, musicien de cour." *Acta* XXXIV (1962), 142–155.

46 n. 33, 78–79

Gombosi

Gombosi, Otto. "French Secular Music of the Fourteenth Century." *MQ* XXXVI (1950), 603–610.

22, 46, 77, 84, 95

Greenberg

Greenberg, Noah. "Early Music Performance Today." *Ree-Fest*, 314–318.

67

Grove

Grove, Sir George. *Dictionary of Music and Musicians.* 5th ed., edited by Erich Blom. London, Macmillan; New York, St. Martin's Press, 1954. 9 vol. and supplement (1960).

Gülke

Gülke, Peter. "Strassburg, Ms. 222, C22." *MGG* XII, 1437–1438.

66

Günther *1*

Günther, Ursula. "Die anonymen Kompositionen des Manuskripts Paris, B.N., fonds it. 568 (Pit)." *AfMW* XXIII (1966), 73–92.

46, 55, 56 n. 44, 97, 105

Günther *2*

———. "Les Colloques de Wégimont." *MF* XIV (1961), 210–213.

22

Günther *3*

———. "Datierbare Balladen des späten 14. Jahrhunderts." *MD* XVI (1962), 151 n. 31.

84

Günther *4*

———. "Das Ende der Ars Nova." *MF* XVI (1963), 105–120.

22–23

Günther 5   ———. "Der Gebrauch des tempus perfectum diminutum in der Handschrift Chantilly 1047." *AfMW* XVII (1960), 288–289.

56

Günther 6   ———. "Das Manuskript Modena, Biblioteca Estense, α.M.5,24 (olim lat. 568 = Mod)." *MD* XXIV (1970), 17–67.

62

Günther 7   ———. "Die Mensuralnotation der Ars Nova in Theorie und Praxis." *AfMW* XIX–XX:1 (1962–63), 9–28.

23, 71, 86

Günther 8   ———. "Zur Biographie einiger Komponisten der Ars subtilior." *AfMW* XXI (1964), 172–199.

84, 95

Günther 9   ———. "Zur Datierung des Madrigals 'Godi Firenze' und der Handschrift Paris, B. N. fonds it. 568 (Pit)." *AfMW* XXIV:2 (May 1967), 99–119.

55, 96, 97

Gullo   Gullo, Salvatore. *Das Tempo in der Musik des XIII. und XIV. Jahrhundert.* Bern, Paul Haupt, 1964. (*Publ. der schweizerischen musikforschenden Gesellschaft.*)

67

Gushee   Gushee, Lawrence. "New Sources for the Biography of Johannes de Muris." *JAMS* XXII (1969), 3–26.

71

Gutmann   Gutmann, Hans. "Der Decamerone des Boccaccio als musikgeschichtliche Quelle." *ZfMW* XI (1928–29), 397–401.

23, 68

Haas   Haas, Robt. *Aufführungspraxis der Musik.* Potsdam, Athenaion, 1931, 93–100.

68, 86, 92

Haberl *1*   Haberl, Franz X. "Bio-bibliographische Notizen über Ugolino von Orvieto." *KJ* Ser. 2, X (1895), 40–49.
71, 99

Haberl 2   ———. "Wilhelm Dufay." *VfMW* I (1885), 397–530.
83

HAM   *Historical Anthology of Music,* Vol. I. Ed. by A. T. Davison and W. Apel. Cambridge, Mass., Harvard University Press, 1947.
85, 88, 104

Hamm   Hamm, Charles E. *A Chronology of the Works of Guillaume Dufay Based on a Study of Mensural Practice.* Princeton, 1964.
83

Handschin *1*   Handschin, Jacques. *Musikgeschichte im Überblick.* Lucerne, Räber & Cie, 1948 (2d. ed. 1964).
23, 38

Handschin 2   ———. "Die Rolle der Nationen in der Musikgeschichte." *SJfMW* V (1931), 25–42.
24, 68

Harman   Harman, Alec. *Mediaeval and Early Renaissance Music.* London, Rockliff, 1958. (*Man and his Music,* I.)
24, 71, 88, 90

Harrison   Harrison, Frank. "Tradition and Innovation in Instrumental Usage, 1100–1450." *ReeFest,* 319–335.
24, 68, 97

HistS   *History of Music in Sound.* Vol. III, pamph. 65. London, Oxford University Press, 1953.
88, 88 90, 98, 98

Hoppin	Hoppin, R. H. and S. Clercx. "Notes biographiques sur quelques musiciens français du XIVe siècle." *Wég*, 163–192.

84

Hüschen *1*	Hüschen, Heinrich. "Beldemandis." *MGG* I, 1575–1579.

71

Hüschen *2*	———. "Jacobus von Lüttich (Jacobus de Leodio . . . Jacques de Liège)." *MGG* VI, 1626–1631.

71

Hüschen *3*	———. "Marchettus von Padua." *MGG* VIII, 1626–1629.

71

Hus	Husmann, Heinrich, ed. *Die mittelalterliche Mehrstimmigkeit.* Köln, Arno-Volk-Verlag, 1954.

40 n. 26, *88, 90, 93, 107*

IMAMI	*Instituzioni e monumenti dell'arte musicale italiana.* Nuova ser. Milano & New York, Ricordi, 1956–1964.

JAMS	*Journal of the American Musicological Society.* Boston, Mass., 1948–.

Johnson	Johnson, Martha. "A Study of Conflicting Key-Signatures in Francesco Landini's Music." *Hamline Studies in Musicology* II. Hamline University, 1947, 27–39.

92

JRB	*Journal of Renaissance and Baroque Music.* Cambridge, Mass., & Rome, 1946–1948. (Superseded by MD.)

Karp	Karp, Theodore. "The Textual Origin of a Piece of Trecento Polyphony." *JAMS* XX (1967), 469–473.

38

Kiesewetter   Kiesewetter, Raphael G. *Geschichte der europäischabendländischen oder unserer heutigen Musik.* Supplement 3. Leipzig, Breitkopf & Härtel, 1846.
90

KJ   *Kirchenmusikalisches Jahrbuch.* Regensburg, 1886–. Title varies.

Königslöw   Königslöw, Annamarie von. *Die italienischen Madrigalisten des Trecento.* Würzburg, Triltsch, 1940.
24, 38, 46, 76, 79, 82, 85, 86, 88, 92, 94, 96, 97, 98, 100, 101

Kornmüller   Kornmüller, Utto. "Musiklehre des Ugolino von Orvieto." *KJ,* Ser. 2, X (1895), 19–40.
72, 99

Korte *1*   Korte, Werner. "La musica nelle città dell' Italia settentrionale dal 1400 al 1425." *RMI* XXXIX (1932), 513–530.
43

Korte 2   ———. *Studien zur Geschichte der Musik in Italien im ersten Viertel des 15. Jahrhunderts.* Kassel, Bärenreiter, 1933.
24, 43, 46, 77, 81, 95, 101, 102

Krohn   Krohn, Ernst C. "*Nova musica* of Johannes Ciconia." *Manuscripta* V:1 (Feb. 1961), 3–16.
81

Kühn   Kühn, Hellmut. "Das Problem der Harmonik in der Musik der Ars Nova." Doctoral dissertation (unpub.?), Saarbrucken, 1970.
72

Kugler   Kugler, M. "Die Tastenmusik im Codex Faenza." Doctoral dissertation, Munich, 1970.
49

Levi   Levi, Eugenia. *Lirica italiana antica.* Firenze, Olschki, 1905.
                        85

LiGotti *1*   LiGotti, Ettore. "L'Ars Nova e il madrigale." *Atti della reale
                       accademia di scienze, lettere e arti di Palermo*, Ser. 4,
                       Vol. IV:2 (1944), 339–389.
                        38

LiGotti 2   ———— and N. Pirrotta. "Paola Tenorista, fiorentino extra
                       moenia." *Estudios dedicados a Menendez Pidal* III (Ma-
                       drid, 1952), 577–606.
                        97

LiGotti *3*   ————. "Per la biografia di due minori musicisti italiani
                       dell 'Ars Nova.' " LiGotti *8*, 98–105.
                        46, 76, 82

LiGotti *4*   ————. "Il più antico polifonista del secolo XIV, Giovanni
                       da Cascia." *Italica* XXIV (1947), 196–200.
                        86

LiGotti 5   ————. *La poesia musicale italiana del secolo XIV.* Palermo,
                       Palumbo, 1944.
                       24, 39, 48, 51, 52, 53, 55, 56, 57, 76, 79, 82, 84, 85, 86, 88, 92,
                                   96, 98, 100, 101, 102

LiGotti 6   ————. "Poesie musicali italiane del sec. XIV." *Atti della
                       reale accademia di scienze, lettere e arti di Palermo*, Ser. 4,
                       Vol. IV:2 (1944), 99–167.
                        39

LiGotti 7   ————. "Una pretesa incoronazione di Francesco Landini."
                       LiGotti *8*, 91–97.
                        92

LiGotti *8*   ————. *Restauri trecenteschi.* Palermo, Palumbo, 1947.
                        24, 76

LiGotti *9*   ———. "Storia e poesia del *Pecorone*." LiGotti *8*, 140–157.
39

Liuzzi *1*   Liuzzi, Fernando. "La ballata e la lauda." CorteA, 62–68.
39

Liuzzi *2*   ———. *La lauda e i primordi della melodia italiana*, Vol. I. Roma, Libreria dello Stato, 1935.
24–25, 26 n. 14, 39

Liuzzi *3*   ———. "Melodie italiane inedite nel Duecento." *Archivum Romanicum* XIV:4 (1930), 327–560.
39

Liuzzi *4*   ———. "Musica e poesia del Trecento nel codice Vaticano Rossiano 215." *Rendiconti della pontificia accademia romana di archaeologia* XIII:1–2 (1937), 59–71.
39, 58

Liuzzi *5*   ———. "Profilo musicale di Jacopone." *La Nuova antologia* (1931), 171–192.
39

Liuzzi *6*   ———. "Le relazioni musicali tra Fiandra e Italia nel secolo XV." *Institut historique belge de Rome*, Bull. XIX (1938), 189–203.
25

Luciani *1*   Luciani, Sebastiano A. "Le ballate ad una voce del Codice Squarcialupi." *Archivi d' Italia*. Ser. 2. Vol. III (1936), 60–66.
39, 51

Luciani *2*   ———. *La musica in Siena*. Siena, Reale accademia senese degli Intronati, 1942.
44

Ludwig *1*   Ludwig, Friedrich. "Geschichte der Mensural-Notation von
                  1250–1460." *SIMG* VI (1904–05), 597–641.
                  25, 43, 44 n. 30, 48, 51, 52, 55, 56, 60, 62, 64, 66, 72, 81, 82, 86,
                              88, 94, 96, 98, 99, 100, 101

Ludwig 2   ———, ed. *Guillaume de Machaut: Musikalische Werke.*
                  Vol. II, Introduction. Leipzig, Breitkopf & Härtel, 1928.
                  48, 52, 55, 57, 60, 62, 64, 66

Ludwig *3*   ———. "Italienische Madrigale, Balladen, und Cacce."
                  Handbuch der Musikgeschichte, ed. by Guido Adler. 2d
                  ed. Vol. I. Berlin, M. Hess, 1930, 276–291.
                  25, 39, 88, *90*, 92, 98

Ludwig *4*   ———. "Die mehrstimmige Musik des 14. Jahrhunderts."
                  SIMG IV (1902–03), 16–69.
                  25, 26 n. 14, 26 n. 16, 48, 51, 57, 68

Ludwig 5   ———. "Musik des Mittelalters in der badischen Kunst-
                  halle Karlsruhe." *ZfMW* V (1922–23), 434–460.
                  90

Main   Main, Alexander. "Lorenzo Masini's Deer Hunt." In *The
                  Commonwealth of Music . . . in Honor of Curt Sachs,* ed.
                  by G. Reese and R. Brandel. New York, Free Press, 1965,
                  130–162.
                  35 n. 22, 39–40, *93*, 94, 101

Mancini   Mancini, Augusto. "Frammenti di un nuovo codice dell'Ars
                  Nova." *Rendiconti dell'accademia nazionale dei Lincei,*
                  Ser. 8, Vol. II (1947), 85–94.
                  54, 76, 77

Marrocco *1*   Marrocco, W. Thomas. "The Ballata, a Metamorphic Form."
                  Acta XXXI (1959), 32–37.
                  40, 54

Marrocco 2 ———. "The Enigma of the Canzone." *Speculum* XXXI (1956), 704–713.

40

Marrocco 3 ———, ed. *Fourteenth-Century Italian Cacce.* 2d ed., rev. [and expanded]. Cambridge, Mass., Mediaeval Academy of America, 1961. (Mediaeval Academy of America, Publication 39.)

3, 40, 40 n. 26, 46, 52 n. 37, *76, 82, 85, 86, 88,* 88, *90, 93, 95, 98, 100,* 100, *101, 103, 107*

Marrocco 4 ———. "The Fourteenth-Century Madrigal: Its Form and Content." *Speculum* XXVI:3 (1951), 449–457.

40

Marrocco 5 ———. "Integrated Devices in the Music of the Italian Trecento." *Cert* III (1970), 411–429.

25–26, 94

Marrocco 6 ———, ed. *Italian Secular Music.* Monaco, Editions de l'Oiseau-Lyre, 1967–. *(PMF,* 6–11.) VI, 1967; VII, 1971; VIII, 1972; IX, X, and XI, forthcoming.

3, 40, 48, 49, 57, 65 n. 53, 68, *76, 77, 78, 79, 80, 81, 82,* 82, *83, 84, 85, 86,* 86, *87,* 87, *88,* 88, *89, 93,* 94, *94, 95,* 96, *96, 98,* 98, *99, 100,* 100, *101, 102, 103, 104, 105*

Marrocco 7 ———, ed. *The Music of Jacopo da Bologna.* Berkeley and Los Angeles, University of California Press, 1954. (University of California Publications in Music, Vol. V.) (First appeared as a doctoral dissertation, University of California at Los Angeles, 1952, under the title "Jacopo da Bologna and His works.")

26 n. 16, 40, 48, 53, 72, *88,* 88

Marrocco 8 ———. "The Newly Discovered Ostiglia Pages of the Vatican Rossi Codex: The Earliest Italian *Ostinato,*" *Acta* XXXIX (1967), 84–91.

58, *107,* 107

Marrocco *9*   ———. "Paolo Tenorista in a new Fragment of the Italian
                    Ars Nova." *JAMS* XV:2 (summer 1962), 213–214.
                                                    97

Martinez *1*   Martinez-Göllner, Marie Louise. "L'Ars Nova italiana del
                    Trecento. . . ." *MF* XVII (1964), 432–433.
                                                    26, 72

Martinez 2   ———. "Marchettus of Padua and Chromaticism." *Cert* III
                    (1970), 187–202.
                                                    72

Martinez *3*   ———. *Die Musik des frühen Trecento.* Tutzing, 1963.
                    (Münchener Veröffentlichungen zur Musikgeschichte, 9.)
                                            26, 40, 58, 72

MD   *Musica Disciplina.* Cambridge, Mass., & Rome, 1948–.
                    (Supersedes *JRB.*)

Meyer-Baer   Meyer-Baer, Kathi. "Music in Dante's *Divina commedia.*"
                    ReeFest, 614–627.
                                                    26

MF   *Die Musikforschung.* Kassel, 1948–.

MGG   *Die Musik in Geschichte und Gegenwart* . . . , ed. by Fried-
                    rich Blume. Kassel & Basel, Bärenreiter, 1949–. 14 vols.
                    and continuing supplements. I, 1949; II, 1952; III, 1954;
                    IV, 1955; V, 1956; VI, 1957; VII, 1958; VIII, 1960; IX,
                    1961; X, 1962; XI, 1963; XII, 1965; XIII, 1966; XIV, 1968.

Mischiati   Mischiati, Oscar. "Uno sconosciuto frammento appartenente
                    al codice Vaticano Rossi 215." *RIM* I:1 (1966), 68–76.
                                                58, 107

ML   *Music and Letters.* London, 1920–.

Monterosso *1*   Monterosso, Raffaello. "Un 'auctoritas' dantesca in un madrigale dell'Ars Nova." *CHM* IV (1966), 185–193.
96, 97

Monterosso 2   ———. "La tradizione melismatica sino al'Ars Nova." *Cert* III (1970), 29–50.
41

Morini   Morini, A. "Un celebre musico dimenticato, Giovanni da Cascia." *Bolletino della regia* . . . (Perugia, 1926), 305 ff.
86

MQ   *The Musical Quarterly.* New York, 1915–.

Musica   *La musica,* ed. by Guido M. Gatti and Alberto Basso. Torino, Unione Tipografico-Editrice (1966–1971). Part I: Enciclopedia storica. 4 vols.; Part II: Dizionario. 2 vols.

NA   *Note d'archivio per la storia musicale.* Rome, 1924–1942.

Nicholson   Nicholson, Edward W. B. "Introduction." In *Dufay and His Contemporaries,* ed. by John, J. F. R., and C. Stainer. London & New York, Novello, 1898, vii–xix.
46, 63, 72, 83

NM   *La Nuova musica.* Florence, 1896–1919.

NOH   *New Oxford History of Music.* Vol. III. London, Oxford University Press, 1960.

Nolthenius *1*   Nolthenius, Hélène. "Een autobiografisch Madrigal van F. Landini." *Tijdschrift voor Muziekwetenschap* XVII (1955), 237–241.
92

Nolthenius 2   ———. *In that Dawn*. London, Longman & Todd, 1968.
                    (Translation from Dutch and German editions.)
                                        26

Novati   Novati, Francesco. "Contributi alla storia della lirica musi-
                   cale neolatina. Per l'origine e la storia della caccia." *Studi
                   medievali* II (1906–07), 303–326.
                                        41, 103

OH   *Oxford History of Music*. . . . 2d ed. London, Oxford Uni-
                   versity Press, 1929–1938. Vol. I, 1929; Vol. II, 1932.
                                        27, 90, 98

Osthoff   Osthoff, Wolfgang. "Petrarca in der Musik Abendlandes."
                   Castrum Peregrini XX (Amsterdam, 1954), 5–19.
                                        41, *88*

PAMS   *Papers of the American Musicological Association*. [Oberlin,
                   O.], 1936–1941.

Parrish *1*   Parrish, Carl. "Giovanni da Firenze: Caccia, 'Con brachi
                   assai.' " ParrishT, 76–78.
                                        41, 87

ParrishM   ———, and J. F. Ohl, eds. *Masterpieces of Music Before
                   1750*. New York, W. W. Norton, 1951.
                                        90

Parrish 2   ———. *The Notation of Medieval Music*. New York, W. W.
                   Norton, 1957.
                                        72

ParrishT   ———, ed. *A Treasury of Early Music*. New York, Norton,
                   1958.
                                        86

Perroy   Perroy, Edouard. "Le point de vue de l'historien." *Wég*, 261–269.

                                                       27

Perz   Perz, Miroslaw. "Die Einflüsse der ausgehenden italienischen Ars Nova in Polen." *Cert* III (1970), 465–483.

                                                       27

Petrobelli   Petrobelli, Pierluigi. "Some Dates for Bartolino da Padova." *Studies in Music History: Essays for Oliver Strunk*, ed. by Harold Powers. Princeton, 1968, 94–112.

                                             46 n. 33, 79

Pirro   Pirro, André. *Histoire de la musique de la fin du XIVe siècle à la fin du XVIe*. Paris, Librairie Renouard, 1940.

                                                       83

Pirrotta *1*   Pirrotta, Nino. "Una arcaica descrizione trecentesca del madrigale." *Festschrift Heinrich Besseler* (Leipzig, 1961), 155–161.

                                                       41

Pirrotta 2   ———. "Ars Nova." *Musica* I:1, 189–197.

                                                      27

Pirrotta *3*   ———. "Ars Nova e stil novo." *RIM* I:1 (1966), 3–19.

                                                     27–28

Pirrotta *4*   ———. "Ballata." *EM* I, 171–173.

                                                      41

Pirrotta *5*   ———. "Ballata." *MGG* I, 1157–1164.

                                                      41

Pirrotta *6*   ———. "Bartolino da Padova." *EM* I, 196.

                                                      79

Pirrotta 7   ———. "Bartolomeo de Bononia." EM I, 196.
                                        79

Pirrotta *8*   ———. "Caccia." *EM* I, 354–355.
                                        41

Pirrotta *9*   ———. "Codex Palatino Panciatichiano 26 (FP)." *MGG* IV,
                      401–405.
                                        52

Pirrotta *10:I*   ——— and E. LiGotti. "Il codice di Lucca." *MD* III (1949),
                      119–138.
                                        47, 53 n. 41, 54, 87

Pirrotta *10:II*   ——— and ———. "Il codice di Lucca." *MD* IV (1950),
                      111–152.
                                        54, *76*, 76, *95*, 96, 97, *100*, 104

Pirrotta *10:III*   ——— and ———. "Il codice di Lucca." *MD* V (1951), 115–
                      142.
                                        51–52, 55, 76, 77, 79, 81, 96, 97, 101, 101 n. 97, 102, 104

Pirrotta *11*   ———. *Il Codice Estense lat. 568 e la musica francese in
                      Italia al principio del 1400.* Palermo, 1946. (Estratto degli
                      *Atti della reale accademia di scienze, lettere e arti di
                      Palermo.* Ser. 4, Vol. V:2.)
                                        45, 62, 64, 77, 79, 95, 101, 101 n. 97

Pirrotta *12*   ———. "Cronologia e denominazione dell'Ars Nova ital-
                      iana." *Wég,* 93–109.
                                        28, 48, 52, 58, 107

Pirrotta *13*   ———. "D⌣natus de Florentia (Dominus)." *MGG* III, 660–
                      661.
                                        82

Pirrotta *14*   ———. "Due sonetti musicali del Trecento." In *Miscelánea en homenaje a monseñor Higinio Anglés*. Vol. II. Barcelona, 1958–1961, 651–662.
18 n. 9, 41

Pirrotta *15*   ———. " 'Dulcedo e subtilitas' nella pratica polifonica franco-italiana al principio del '400." *RB* II:3–4 (1948), 125–132.
28, 62

Pirrotta *16*   ———. "Gherardellus de Florentia." *MGG* V, 55–57.
85

Pirrotta *17*   ———. "Italien. B) 14–16 Jahrhundert." *MGG* VI, 1476–1480.
28

Pirrotta *18*   ———. "Jacobus de Bononia." *MGG* VI, 1619–1625.
88

Pirrotta *19*   ———. "Johannes de Florentia." *MGG* VII, 90–92.
87

Pirrotta *20*   ———. "Landini (Landino), Francesco." *MGG* VIII, 163–168.
92

Pirrotta *21*   ———. "Laurentius de Florentia." *MGG* VIII, 332–333.
94

Pirrotta *22*   ———. "Lirica monodica trecentesca." *RaM* IX (1936), 317–325.
28, 58, 85, 94, 96

Pirrotta *23*   ———. "Das Madrigal der Ars Nova: Etymologie, formale Gestaltung, und Geschichte." *MGG* VIII, 1419–1424.
41–42

Pirrotta *24*   ———. "Il madrigale e la caccia." CorteA, 57–61.
                                        28, 42

Pirrotta *25*   ———. "Marchettus de Padua and the Italian Ars Nova."
                         MD IX (1955), 51–71.
                                  28–29, 44, 45, 50 n. 36, 52, 58

Pirrotta *26*   ———, ed. *The Music of Fourteenth-Century Italy.* Rome,
                         American Institute of Musicology, 1954–1964. 5 vols.
                         (*CMM* VIII: 1–5.) I, 1954; II, 1960; III, 1962; IV, 1963;
                         V, 1964.
                         3, 29, 40 n. 26, 45, 47, 52 n. 37, 53, 57, 58, 63 n. 52, *76, 76,*
                         81, 82 *82, 85,* 85, *86*, 86 *87*, 87, *88, 89,* 89, *93*, 94, *98*, 98, *99,*
                         99, *100*, 100, *104*, 104, *105*, 106, *106*, 107, *107*, 107 n. 109

Pirrotta *27*   ———. "Musica polifonica per un testo attributo a Federico
                         II." *Cert* II (1968), 97–108.
                                        42, *105*, 106

Pirrotta *29*   ———. "Note su un codice di antiche musiche per tastiera."
                         RMI LVI (1954), 333–339.
                                              68

Pirrotta *30*   ———. On Text Forms from Ciconia to Dufay." *ReeFest,*
                         673–682.
                                         42, 83, 93

Pirrotta *31*   ———. "Paolo da Firenze in un nuovo frammento dell'Ars
                         Nova." *MD* X (1956), 61–66.
                                              97

Pirrotta *33*   ———, ed. *Paolo Tenorista in a New Fragment of the
                         Italian Ars Nova.* Palm Springs, California, E. E. Gottlieb,
                         1961.
                         44, 48, 53, 55, 55 n. 43, 58, 62, *96*, 97, 105 n. 105, 107 n. 109

Pirrotta *34* ————. "Per l'origine e la storia della caccia e del madrigale trecentesco." *RMI* XLVIII (1946), 305–323; XLIX (1947), 121–142.

26 n. 16, 40 n. 27, 42, 42 n. 29, 98 n. 91

Pirrotta *35* ————. "Piero e l'impressionismo musicale del secolo XIV." *Cert* I (1962), 57–74.

42, 98–99

Pirrotta *36* ————, and LiGotti. *Il Sacchetti e la tecnica musicale del Trecento italiano*. Firenze, G. C. Sansoni, 1935. With musical supplement.

29, 42, 48, 87, *87*, 89, *90*, *93*, *95*, 96, 97, 101, 102

Pirrotta *37* ————. "Scuole polifoniche italiane durante il secolo XIV: Di una pretesa scuola napolitana." *CHM* I (1953), 11–18.

44, 77

Pirrotta *38* ————. "Sull'etimologia di 'madrigale.'" *Poesia* IX (1948), 60–61.

42

Pirrotta *39* ————. "Tradizione orale e tradizione scritta della musica." *Cert* III (1970), 431–439.

29

PJ *Peters. Jahrbuch der Musikbibliothek Peters*. Leipzig, 1894– 1940. Superseded by *Deutsches Jahrbuch der Musikwissenschaft*.

Plamenac *1* Plamenac, Dragan. "Alcune osservazioni sulla struttura del codice 117 della biblioteca comunale di Faenza." *Cert* III (1970), 161–175.

49, 68

Plamenac 2 ————. "Another Paduan Fragment of Trecento Music." *JAMS* VIII (1955), 165–181.

60 n. 49, 61, 64, 89, 92

Plamenac 3   ———. "Faenza, Codex 117." *MGG* III, 1709–1714.
                                                49, 68

Plamenac 4   ———. "Faventina." In *Liber Amicorum Charles Van den
                  Borren*, ed. by Albert Van der Linden. Anvers, Lloyd
                  Anversois, 1964, 145–164.
                                        49–50, 68, 89, *103*, 103

Plamenac 5   ———. "Keyboard Music of the Fourteenth Century in
                  Codex Faenza 117." *JAMS* IV (1951), 179–201.
                                                50, 68

Plamenac 6   ———. "New Light on the Codex Faenza 117." *RIMS*
                  (Utrecht, 1952), 310–326.
                                                50, 68, *100*

Plamenac 7   ———. "A Note on the Rearrangement of the Faenza Codex
                  117." *JAMS* XVII: 1 (spring 1964), 78–81.
                                                50

PMA   *Proceedings of the Musical Association.* London, 1874–1943.
                  Superseded by *PRMA*.

PMF   *Polyphonic Music of the Fourteenth Century*, ed. by Leo
                  Schrade and Frank L. Harrison. Monaco, Editions de
                  l'Oiseau-Lyre, 1956–.

PRMA   *Proceedings of the Royal Musical Association.* London,
                  1944–.

Quadrivium   *Quadrivium. Rivista di filologia e musicologiia medievale.*
                  Bologna, 1956–. Title varies.

Quadrivium, s.m. [*Quadrivium*] *Biblioteca di "Quadrivium." Serie musico-
                  logica.* Bologna, Forni, 1957–. (Reprints of *Quadrivium*.)

RaM   *Rassegna musicale.* Turin, 1928–1962.

RB   *Revue belge de musicologie.* Antwerp, 1946–.

Reaney *1*   Reaney, Gilbert. "Ars Nova." In *Pelican History of Music,*
                       ed. by A. Robertson and Denis Stevens. Vol. I. Penguin
                       Books, 1960, 261–308.
                            29–30, 42, 76, 77, 79, 81, 94 n. 83, 101

Reaney 2   ———. "The *Ars Nova* of Philippe de Vitry." *MD* X (1956),
                       5–33.
                                           72

Reaney *3*   ———. "Bodleian Library . . . Canonici Misc 213 (O) [Ox-
                       forder Handschriften]." *MGG* X, 517–518.
                                           63

Reaney *4*   ———. "Egidius de Murino (de Morino, de Muris, de
                       Mori)." *MGG* III, 1169–1172.
                                           84

Reaney *5*   ———. "Franciscus." *MGG* II, 634–636.
                                           85

Reaney *6*   ———. "The Italian Contribution to the Manuscript Ox-
                       ford, Bodleian Library, Canonici Misc. 213." *Cert* III
                       (1970), 443–464.
                            47, 63, 77, 79, 80, 82, 84, 93, 94, 98, 99, 101–102

Reaney 7   ———. "The Manuscript London, B.M., Additional 29987
                       (Lo)." *MD* XII (1958), 67–91.
                                   53, 53 n. 39, 82, 99

Reaney *8*   ———, ed. *The Manuscript London, B.M., Additional
                       29987, A Facsimile Edition.* (n.p.) American Institute of

Musicology, 1965. (*Musicological Studies and Documents,* 13.)

53

Reaney *9*   ———. "The Manuscript Oxford, Bodleian Library Canonici misc. 213." *MD* IX (1955), 73–104.

63, 63 n. 51, 80, 82, 99

Reaney *10*   ———. "The Manuscript Paris, Bibliothèque Nationale, fonds italien 568 (Pit)." *MD* XIV (1960), 33–63.

55, 78, 82, 85, 86, 90

Reaney *11*   ———. "Matteo da Perugia (Matheus de Perusio)." *MGG* VIII, 1793–1794.

95

Reaney *12*   ———. "The Middle Ages." In *A History of Song,* ed. by Denis Stevens. 2d ed. New York, W. W. Norton, 1970, 37–62.

30, 43, 68, 76, 81, 84, 85, 87, 89, 92, 95, 96, 101

Reaney *13*   ———. "Pariser Handschriften." *MGG* X, 796–797.

56, 57

Reaney *14*   ———. "The Performance of Medieval Music." *ReeFest,* 704–722.

68, 87

Reaney *15*   ———. "Studien zur italienischen Musik des Trecento und frühen Quattrocento. . . ." *ML* XXXVII (1956), 392–394. A review of Fischer *32.*

30

Reaney *16*   ———. "Die wichtige Trecento-Hs. *Add 29987 (Lo)*. . . ." *MGG* VIII, 1185–1187.

53

Reaney *17*   ———. "Zachara und Zacharias." *MGG* XIV, 960–963.
                                    101, 102

ReeFest   [Reese Festschrift] *Aspects of Medieval and Renaissance Music: A Birthday Offering to Gustave Reese,* ed. by Jan LaRue. New York, W. W. Norton, 1966.

ReeM   Reese, Gustave. *Music in the Middle Ages.* New York, W. W. Norton, 1940.
                            4, 30, 43, *88, 90,* 92, 96, 102

ReeR   ———. *Music in the Renaissance.* 2d ed. New York, W. W. Norton, 1959.
                            30, 77, 79, 80, 81, 82 n. 71, 84, 95, 102

Rehm   Rehm, Wolfgang. "Lantins (Lantinis, Latinis, Lantius, Lanetius), Hugo (Hugho, Ugo) de." *MGG* VIII, 200–202.
                                    93

Riemann *1*   Riemann, Hugo. "Florenz, die Wiege der Ars Nova." Riemann 2, I:2, 297–335.
                            30–31, 67, 69

Riemann 2   ———. *Handbuch der Musikgeschichte.* Leipzig, Breitkopf & Härtel, 1904–1913. 2 vols. in 5 (2d ed. 1920–23).
                            85, 86, 88, 90

RiemannHaus   ———, ed. *Hausmusik aus alter Zeit.* Leipzig, Breitkopf & Härtel, 1906.
                                    96

Riemann *4*   ———. "Das Kunstlied im 14.–15. Jahrhundert." *SIMG* VII (1905–6), 529–550.
                            31, 89, 97, 99

RiemannMB   ————, ed. *Musikgeschichte in Beispielen*. Leipzig, E. A. Seeman, 1925.

86, 91

RiemannML   ————. *Musiklexikon*. 12th ed. Mainz, Schott, 1959. 2 vols.

RIM   *Rivista italiana di musicologia*. Milano, 1964–. (Supersedes *RMI*.)

RIMS   *Reports of the International Musicological Society*. 1930–. (Title and place vary.)

RMI   *Rivista musicale italiana*. Turin, 1898–1955. (Superseded by *RIM*.)

Roncaglia   Roncaglia, Gino. "Intorno ad un codice di Johannes Bonadies." *Atti e memorie della reale accademia di scienze, lettere ed arti di Modena*, Ser. 5, Vol. IV (1939), 39 ff.

50

Sabbadini   Sabbadini, Remiglio. "Frammenti di poesie volgari musicate," *Giornale storico della letteratura italiana* XL (1902), 270.

61, 102 n. 100

Sachs   Sachs, Kurt. *Rhythm and Tempo: A Study in Music History*. New York, 1953.

31, 69, 72

Sartori *1*   Sartori, Claudio. "Matteo da Perugia e Bertrand Feragut." *Acta* XXVIII (1956), 12–27.

95

Sartori 2   ————. *La notazione italiana del Trecento*. Firenze, Olschki, 1938.

72

Schachter   Schachter, Carl. "Landini's Treatment of Consonance and Dissonance: A Study in Fourteenth-Century Counterpoint." *Music Forum* II (1970), 130–186.
92

Schering *1*   Schering, Arnold. *Aufführungspraxis alter Musik.* Leipzig, Quelle & Meyer, 1931, 16–18.
69

Schering *2*   ———. "Ars Antiqua e Ars Nova." CorteA, 42–46.
31

ScheringGB   ———, ed. *Geschichte der Musik in Beispielen.* Leipzig, Breitkopf & Härtel, 1931.
86, 91

Schering *4*   ———. "Das kolorierte Orgelmadrigal des Trecento." *SIMG* XIII (1911–12), 172–204.
67, 69

Schering *5*   ———. *Studien zur Musikgeschichte der Frührenaissance.* Leipzig, C. F. Kant Nachfolger, 1914.
31–32, 69, *86, 95*

Schneider *1*   Schneider, Marius. *Die Ars Nova des XIV Jahrhunderts in Frankreich und Italien.* Wolfenbüttel-Berlin, Kallmeyer, 1930.
32

Schneider 2   ———. "Das gestalttypologische Verfahren in der Melodik des Francesco Landino." *Acta* XXXV (1963), 2–14.
32, 92

Schneider *3*   ———. "Klagelieder des Volkes in der Kunstmusik der italienischen Ars Nova." *Acta* XXXIII (1961), 162–168.
32

Schrade *1*   Schrade, Leo. "The Chronology of the Ars Nova in France."
                   Wég, 36–62.
                                        32, 81

Schrade *2*   ———, ed. *The Works of Francesco Landini*. Monaco, Edi-
                   tions de l'Oiseau-Lyre, 1958. (*PMF* 4.) (With separate com-
                   mentary.)
                                   32, 53, *90*, 92–93

Seay *1*   Seay, Albert. "The *Declaratio musice discipline* of Ugolino
                   of Orvieto: Addenda." *MD* XI (1957), 126–133.
                                        72

Seay *2*   ———. *Music in the Medieval World*. Englewood Cliffs,
                   N.J., Prentice-Hall, 1965.
                                     33, 43, 93

Seay *3*   ———. "Paolo da Firenze: A Trecento Theorist." *Cert* I
                   (1962), 118–140.
                                      72, 97

Seay *4*   ———. "Ugolino da Orvieto." *EM* IV, 444.
                                        72

Seay *5*   ———. "Ugolino of Orvieto, theorist and composer." *MD*
                   IX (1955), 111–166.
                                        73

Seay *6*   ———. "Ugolino von Orvieto." *MGG* XIII, 1022–1023.
                                     73, *99*, 100

Sesini   Sesini, Ugo. "Il canzoniero musicale trecentesco del cod. Vat.
                   Rossiano 215." *Studi medievali* (N.S.) XVI (1943–50), 212–
                   236.
                                        58

SIMG   *Sammelbände der internationalen Musikgesellschaft.* Leipzig,
                     1899–1914.

SJfMW   *Schweizerisches Jahrbuch für Musikwissenschaft.* Basel, 1924–
                     1938.

Smith *1*   Smith, F. Joseph. "Ars Nova—a Redefinition?" *MD* XVIII
                     (1964), 19–35; XIX (1965), 83–97.
                                          33

Smith 2   ———. *Iacobi Leodiensis "Speculum musicae": A Com-
                     mentary.* 2 vols. Brooklyn, Institute of Mediaeval Music,
                     1966–69. (Musicological Studies, 13, 22).
                                          73

Stainer   Stainer, Sir John, J. F. R., and C., eds. *Dufay and His Con-
                     temporaries.* London and New York, Novello, 1898.
                     (Early Bodleian Music.) (With an important introduction
                     by E. W. B. Nicholson.)
                             63, 69, 73, *79, 82,* 84, *99*

Steiner   Steiner, M. "Ein Beitrag zur Notationsgeschichte des frühen
                     Trecento: Die Lehren des Marchettus von Padua und der
                     Codex Rossian 215." Unpublished doctoral dissertation,
                     Vienna, 1931.
                                       58, 73

Stellfeld   Stellfeld, Bent. "Prosdocimus de Beldomandis als Erneuerer
                     der Musikbetrachtung um 1400." In *Natalica musicologica
                     Knud Jeppesen,* ed. by Bjorn Hjelmborg and Søren Søren-
                     sen. Hafnia, W. Hansen, 1962, 37–50.
                                          73

Strunk *1*   Strunk, Oliver. "Intorno a Marchetto da Padova." *RaM* XX
                     (1950), 312–315.
                                      33, 58, 73

Strunk 2   ——, ed. *Source Readings in Music History; Antiquity and the Middle Ages.* New York, Norton, 1950.

73

Taucci   Taucci, Raffaello. *Fra Andrea dei Servi, organista e compositore del Trecento.* Roma, Collegio S. Alessio Falconieri, 1935. (Estratto dalla *Rivista di studi storici sull'Ordine dei Servi di Maria*, A.II, 1935.)

52, 53, 76, 76

\# Termini   Termini, Francesco. "Don Paolo." Unpublished doctoral dissertation, University of Southern California, 1956.

97

Thibault   Thibault, Geneviève. "Emblèmes et devises des Visconti dan les oeuvres musicales du Trecento." *Cert* III (1970), 131–160.

46 n. 33, 47, 56

Toguchi *1*   Toguchi, Kosaku. "Studio sul Codice Rossiano 215 della biblioteca vaticana; intorno al sistema della sua notazione musicale." *Annuario dell instituto giapponese di cultura* I (Rome, 1963), 169–184.

58, 73

Toguchi 2   ——. "Sulla struttura e l'esecuzione di alcune cacce italiane; un cenno sulle origini delle cacce arsnovistiche." *Cert* III (1970), 67–81.

43, 98, 99

Torchi   Torchi, Luigi, ed. *L'arte musicale in Italia.* Vol. I. Milano, Ricordi, 1897.

88

Van   Van, Guillaume de. "Inventory of the Manuscript Bologna Liceo Musicale, Q 15 (olim 37)." *MD* II (1948). 231–257.

60

Vecchi *1* Vecchi, Giuseppe, ed. *Il canzoniere musicale del Codice Vaticano Rossi 215 con uno studio sulla melica italiana del Trecento.* Vol. I. Bologna, Università degli studi di Bologna, 1965. (Monumenta lyrica medii aevi italica, 3.) Facsimile edition.

58

Vecchi 2 ———. "Letteratura e musica nel Trecento." *Cert* III (1970), 485–503.

33

Vecchi *4* ———. *Su la composizione del "Pomerium" di Marchetto da Padova e la "Brevis compilatio."* Bologna, 1957. (*Quadrivium, s.m.,* 1.)

73

Vecchi 5 ———. "Teorie e prassi nel canto a due voci in Italia nel Duecento e nel primo Trecento." *Cert* III (1970), 203–214.

33–34

Vecchi 6 ———. "Tra monodia e polifonia." *CHM* II (1957), 447–464.

34, 43

VfMW *Vierteljahrschrift für Musikwissenschaft.* Leipzig, 1885–1894.

Villani Villani, Philippi. *Liber de origine civitatis Florentiae et eiusdem famosis civibus,* ed. by G. C. Galletti. Firenze, 1847.

44, 47, 87, 93, 94

Ward Ward, John. "W. Thomas Marrocco's *The Music of Jacopo da Bologna.*" *JAMS* VIII (1955), 36–41.

89

Wég Les Colloques de Wégimont II, 1955. *L'Ars Nova: recueil d'études sur la musique du XIVe siècle.* Paris, Société d'Edition "Les belles lettres," 1959.

Wesselofsky   Wesselofsky, Alessandro, ed. *"Il paradiso degli Alberti" di Giovanni da Prato.* Bologna, Romagnoli, 1867. 3 vols.
                     18 n.8, 18 n. 9 34, 44, 93

\# White   White, John Reeves. "Music of the Early Italian Ars Nova." Doctoral dissertation, University of Indiana, 1952. 2 vols.
                     34

Wilkins *1*   Wilkins, Nigel. "The Codex Reina: A Revised Description." *MD* XVII (1963), 57–73.
                     57

Wilkins *2*   ———, ed. *A Fourteenth-Century Repertory from the Codex Reina.* American Institute of Musicology, 1966. (*CMM, 36.*)
                     57

Wilkins *3*   ———. "A Madrigal in Praise of the Della Scala Family." *RB* XIX (1965), 82–88.
                     47, *105*, 106

Wolf *1*   Wolf, Johannes. "L'arte del biscanto misurato secondo il maestro Jacopo da Bologna." In *Theodor Kroyer Festschrift.* (Regensburg, 1933), 17–39.
                     73

Wolf *2*   ———. "Dufay und seine Zeit." *SIMG* I (1899–1900), 150–163.
                     47, 63, 73, 94

Wolf *3*   ———. "Firenze musicale nel '300." CorteA, 46–50.
                     34, 45

Wolf *4*   ———. "Florenz in der Musikgeschichte des 14. Jahrhunderts." *SIMG* III (1901–02), 599–646.
                     34, 45, 47, 73, *82*, *85*, *86*, *91*, 93, *96*, *98*, *101*

Wolf 5   ————. *Geschichte der Mensural-Notation von 1250–1460.* Leipzig, Breitkopf & Härtel, 1904. 3 vols. I Historical text, with illustrations; II Music in old notation; III Transcriptions of Vol. II.

34–35, 40 n. 26, 47, 48, 52, 53, 56, 57, 60, 62, 64, 65, 66, 73, *78, 78, 79, 79, 82, 86, 88,* 90, *91, 93, 95, 96, 98, 99,* 99, *100, 101*

Wolf 6   ————. *Handbuch der Notationskunde.* Leipzig, Breitkopf & Härtel, 1913–1919. 2 vols.

74, *86, 88*

Wolf 7   ————. "Intorno ad alcune musiche profane italiane del secolo XIV." *NM* I:2 (Dec. 1897), [?]–75.

35, 48

Wolf 8   ————. "Italian Trecento Music." *PMA* LVIII (1931), 15–31.

35, 69

WolfME   ————, ed. *Music of Earlier Times.* New York, Broude Bros., 1930. (American reprint of *Sing-und Spielmusik aus älterer Zeit,* the collection of musical examples from Wolf 5.)

91, 95

Wolf 10   ————. "Musica fiorentina nel secolo XIV." *NM,* supplements I–III.

76, 82, 85, 86, 91, 93, 96, 98

Wolf 11   ————. "La notazione italiana nel secolo XIV." *NM* II:4 (Oct. 1899), 73–75.

74

Wolf 12   ————. "Die Rossi Handschrift 215 der Vaticana und das Trecento Madrigal." *PJ* XLV (1938), 53–69.

43, 59, 69, *93, 107,* 107

WolfSS   ————, ed. *Sing und Spielmusik aus älterer Zeit.* Leipzig, Quelle & Meyer, 1926.

91, 95

WolfSq   ————, and H. Albrecht, eds. *Der Squarcialupi-Codex, Pal.*
                    87 der biblioteca Medicea Laurenziana zu Florenz. . . .
                    Lippstadt, Kistner & Siegel, 1955.
                    35–36, 40 n. 26, 47, 48, 55 *76,* 76, *78,* 82, *82, 84, 85, 86,* 87, *88,*
                                    90, 93, *93, 95, 100,* 102

Wolff   Wolff, Hellmuth C. "Dufay, Guillaume." *EM* II, 99–100.
                                    84

Wouters, Jos.   Wouters,   Jos.   *Harmonische   Verschijningsvormen   in   de*
                    Muziek van de XIIIe tot de XVIe Eeuw. [Amsterdam?
                    1954?]
                                    62, 63, 74, 81, 87, 93, 95, 96, 99

ZfMW   *Zeitschrift für Musikwissenschaft.* Leipzig, 1918–1935. (Su-
                    perseded by *AfMF.*)

Appendix II

Literary Supplement[114]

⟨✕⟩

Ancona, see D'Ancona

Antognoni, Oreste. "Le glosse ai documenti d'amore di M. Francesco da Barberino." *Giornale di filologia romanza* IV (1892), 78–98.

Antonio da Tempo, see Tempo, Antonio da

Bertoni, Giulio. *I trovatori d'Italia.* Modena, Orlandini, 1915.

Biadene, Leandro. "Madrigale." *Rassegna bibliografica della letteratura italiana* VI (1898), 329–336.

Cappelli, Antonio. *Poesie musicali anonime tratte dal codice Mediceo-Laurenziana (Palat. 87).* Modena, 1871.

————. *Poesie musicali dei secoli XIV, XV, XVI.* Bologna, Romagnoli, 1868.

Carducci, Giosuè. *Antica lirica italiana.* Firenze, 1907.

————, ed. *Cacce in rima dei secoli XIV e XV.* Bologna, Zanichelli, 1896.

————, ed. *Cantilene e ballate, strambotti e madrigali nei secoli XIII e XIV.* Pisa, Nistri, 1871.

————. *Della lirica popolare italiana del secolo XIII e XIV,* in his *Opere* **XVIII.**

————. "Musica e poesia nel mondo elegante italiano del secolo XIV." In his *Studi letterari.* Bologna, Zanichelli, 1929, 301–397.

OR

————. *Musica e poesia nel mondo elegante italiano del secolo XIV.* In his *Opere* VIII. Bologna, Zanichelli, 1893.

————, ed. *Rime di Cino da Pistoja e d'altri del secolo XIV.* Firenze, 1862.

Casini, Tommaso. *Le forme metriche italiane.* Firenze, G. C. Sansoni, 1890.

114. Many of these entries are directly related to Forms (Section II), and several of them serve as primary sources as well (Section IV). For this reason there are a number of duplications.

Chaytor, Henry J. *The Troubadours of Dante.* Oxford, Clarendon Press, 1902.

Corsi, Giuseppe, ed. *Poesie musicali del Trecento.* Bologna, Commissione per i testi di lingua, 1970.

D'Ancona, A. *La poesia popolare italiana.* Livorno, 1907.

D'Angeli, Andrea. *La musica ai tempi di Dante.* Caglieri, 1903.

Debenedetti, Santorre. "Un trattatello del secolo XIV sopra la poesia musicale." *Studi medievali* II (1906–07), 59–82.

Devoto, Giacomo. "Dalla lingua latina alla lingua di Dante." *Il Trecento.* Firenze, 1953.

Flamini, F. *La lirica toscana del Rinascimento anteriore ai tempi del Magnifico.* Pisa, Nistri, 1891. (*Annali della Scuola normale di Pisa,* 14.)

Gidel, Charles. *Les troubadours et Pétrarque.* Angers, 1857.

Giustiniani, Leonardo. *Poesie edite e inedite . . . ,* ed. by Weise. Bologna, 1883.

Levi, Eugenia, comp. *Lirica italiana antica.* Firenze, Olschki, 1906.

Levi, Ezio. *Poesia di popolo e poesia di corte nel Trecento.* Livorno, 1915.

LiGotti, Ettore. *La poesia musicale italiana del secolo XIV.* Palermo, Palumbo, 1944.

———. *Restauri trecenteschi.* Palermo, Palumbo, 1947.

——— and Nino Pirrotta. *Il Sacchetti e la tecnica musicale del Trecento italiano.* Firenze, Sansoni, 1935.

Liuzzi, Fernando. "Profilo musicale di Jacopone." *La Nuova antologia* (Sept. 1931), 171–192.

Lovarini, Emilio. "Giosuè Carducci 'Cacce in rima dei secc. XIV e XV.'" *Rassegna bibliografica della letteratura italiana* V (1897), 132–141.

Meierhans, Lydia. *Die Ballata.* Zürich, Juris-Verlag, 1956. (Doctoral dissertation, University of Zürich.)

Miraglia, Yolanda. *La vita e le rime di Niccolò Soldanieri.* Palermo, Pezzino e Figlio, 1947.

Prudenzani, Simone. *Il "Solazzo" e il "Saporetto" con altre rime . . . ,* ed. by S. Debenedetti. Torino, 1913 (*Giornale storico della letteratura italiana,* suppl. no. 15)

Sacchetti, Franco. *Il libro delle rime,* ed. by Gigli. Lucca, Franco e Majorchi, 1853. (Also ed. by A. Chiari. Bari, Laterza, 1936.)

Sapegno, Natalino. *Poeti minori del Trecento.* Milano, Ricciardi, 1952.

Sommacampagna, Gidino da. *Trattato dei ritmi volgari,* ed. by G. B. C. Giuliari. (*Scelta di curiosità letterarie,* CV, 1870.)

Tempo, Antonio da. *Trattato delle rime volgari,* ed. by G. Grion. Bologna, Romagnoli, 1869.

Trucchi, Francesco, comp. *Poesie italiane inedite di Dugento autori. . . .* Prato, Guasti, 1846.

Volpi, G. *Rime di Trecentisti minori.* Firenze, 1907.

Appendix III

Principal Theoretical Treatises [115]

෨෨෨

---

115. The reader is advised to study all introductory notes preceding the treatises.
116. Here attributed to Johannes de Muris.

Philippus de Vitry. *Ars Nova.*[117]   CouS III, 13–
                                                    CSM VIII (Reaney et
                                                    al.)

Prosdocimus de Beldemandis. *Opera. I. Expositiones*   Ed. F. Alberto Gallo.
tractatus pratice cantus mensurabilis Magistri Jo-   Bologna, 1966. (*Anti-*
hannis de Muris.   *quae Musicae Italicae*
                                                         Scriptores, 3)

Prosdocimus de Beldemandis. *Tractatus practicae de*   CouS III, 228–
musica mensurabili ad modum italicorum.   Sartori 2, 35–

Ugolinus d'Orvieto. *Declaratio musice discipline.*   *CSM* VII (Seay)

---

117. See n. 55, p. 72.

Appendix IV

Primary Sources

⊙

Barberino, Francesco da. *Del reggimento e costumi di donna,* ed. by C. Bandi di Vesme. Bologna, Romagnoli, 1875.

————. *I documenti d'amore,* ed. by F. Egidi. Roma, 1902/07. See also O. Antognoni. "Le glosse ai documenti d'amore di M. Francesco da Barberino." *Giornale di folologia romanza* IV (1892), 78–98.

Boccaccio, Giovanni. *Decamerone,* ed. by V. Branca. Firenze, Le Monnier, 1951/52. English translation by R. Aldington. New York, Dell Paperbacks, 1949.

————. *Vita di Dante,* ed. by P. Ricci. Milano, Ricciardi, 1965.

Prato, Giovanni da. *Il Paradiso degli Alberti,* ed. by A. Wesselofsky. Bologna, Romagnoli, 1867.

Prudenzani, Simone. *Il "Solazzo" e il "Saporetto" con altre rime . . . ,* ed. by S. Debenedetti. Torino, 1913 (*Giornale storico della letteratura italiana,* suppl. no. 15)

Sacchetti, Franco. *Novelle,* ed. by O. Gigli. Firenze, Le Monnier, 1860/61.

Salutati, Coluccio. *Epistolario,* ed. by F. Novati. Roma, Istituto storico italiano, 1893.

Sercambi, Giovanni. *Le chroniche di Giovanni Sercambi,* ed. by S. Bongi. Roma, Tip. Giusti, 1892.

————. *Novelle,* ed. by A. D'Ancona. Bologna, 1871.

Villani, Philippi. *Liber de origine civitatis Florentiae et eiusdem famosis civibus,* ed. by G. Galletti. Firenze, 1847.

Postscript

CRWA

Apel, Willi. *Geschichte der Orgel-und Klaviermusik bis 1700.* New York, Bären-reiter, 1967, 25 ff. (V b) (VI) (English translation: *The History of Keyboard Music to 1700.* Indiana University Press, 1972)

Bank, J. A. *Tactus, Tempo and Notation in Mensural Music from the 13th to the 17th Century.* Amsterdam, Annie Bank, 1972, 53 ff. (VII)

Baumann, Dorothea. "Die dreistimmige Satztechnik bei Francesco Landini." Doctoral dissertation (in preparation). Zürich, 1973. (VIII a)

Bisogni, Fabio. "Precisazioni sul Casella dantesco." In *Memorie e contributi alla musica dal medio evo all'età moderna offerti a Federico Ghisi nel suo settantesimo compleanno.* Vol. I. Bologna, 1972. (*Antiquae Musicae Italicae Studiosi*) (I)

D'Accone, Frank A. "Music and Musicians at the Florentine Monastery of Santa Trinità, 1360–1363." In *Memorie e contributi . . . offerti a Federico Ghisi nel suo settantesimo compleanno.* Vol. I. Bologna, 1972. (*Antiquae Musicae Italicae Studiosi*) (*IV*)

Fischer, Kurt von and Max Lütolf. *Handschriften mit mehrstimmiger Musik des 14., 15., und 16. Jahrhunderts. RISM, B/IV, 3 and 4* München, 1972. (V)

———. "Die Musik des Trecento." *Das Trecento.* Zürich, 1960, 185–214. (I)

———. "Zum Wort-Ton Problem in der Musik des italienischen Trecento." In *Festschrift Arnold Geering zum 70. Geburtstag.* Bern, 1972. (I)

Gallo, F. Alberto. "Due trattatelli sulla notazione del primo Trecento." In *Memorie e contributi . . . offerti a Federico Ghisi nel suo settantesimo compleanno.* Vol. I Bologna, 1972. (*Antiquae Musicae Italicae Studiosi*) (*VII*)

————. "Philological Works on Musical Treatises of the Middle Ages. A Bibliographical Report." *Acta* XLIV:1 (1972), 86–94. (VII)

Ghisi, Federico. *Studi e testi di musica italiana dall'Ars Nova a Carissimi.* Bologna, 1972 (*Antiquae Musicae Italicae Studiosi*), 11–145. (I)
A collection of writings which have appeared over a period of some thirty years in various journals.

Guaitamacchi, Valeria, ed. *Madrigali trecenteschi del frammento "Greggiati" di Ostiglia.* Bologna, 1970 (*Quadrivium,* serie paleografica, 9). (VIII b)

Hammerstein, Reinhold. "Die Musik in Dantes *Divina Commedia.*" *Deutsches Dante-Jahrbuch* XLI/XLII (1964), 59–125. (Appendix II)

Heinemann, Siegfried. "Poesia und musica in Dantes Schrift 'De vulgari eloquentia'." In *Festschrift Arnold Geering zum 70. Geburtstag.* Bern, 1972, 41–52. (Appendix II)

Hibberd, Lloyd. "On Instrumental Style in Early Melody." *MQ* XXXII (1946), 107–130. (VI)

Marrocco, W. Thomas and Robert Huestis. "Some Speculations Concerning the Instrumental Music of the Faenza Codex 117." *The Diapason* LXIII:5 (April 1972), 3, 16–19. (V b) (VI)

Nolthenius, Hélène. "De oudste Melodiek van Italië; een Studie over de Muziek van het Dugento." Doctoral dissertation. Utrecht, 1948. (I)

————. *Renaissance in Mei, Florentine leven rond Landino.* Utrecht, 1956. (I) (VIII a)

Pirrotta, Nino. "Zacaras musicus." In *Memorie e contributi . . . offerti a Federico Ghisi nel suo settantesimo compleanno.* Vol. I Bologna, 1972. (*Antiquae Musicae Italicae Studiosi*) (VIII a)

Testi, Flavio. *La musica italiana nel medioevo e nel rinascimento.* Vol. I. Milano, Bramante Editrice, 1969, 109–236. (I)

Index

⟨∞W∞⟩

The Index provides ample coverage for pages 1–74. However, pages 9–11 are excluded, since these serve as an index to the manuscripts. With few exceptions, indexing of the Transcriptions section (pages 75–108) is confined to composer names and text incipits. Text incipits beginning with the definite or indefinite article are alphabetized by the article, in keeping with the practice of most Trecento scholars. In the text the names of Giovanni, Jacopo, and Paolo often stand alone. In such cases it is to be assumed that these refer to Giovanni da Cascia, Jacopo da Bologna, and Paolo da Firenze. Variations in names and in spelling of some words are indicated with parentheses, and in some cases with cross references.